Welcome to the United States of America

1 Describe the pictures ▸ *pp. 6–7*

○* ***a)*** *Which words describe the pictures on pp. 6–7 of your student's book? Which words don't describe the pictures? First, write the words correctly.*

gdernasuo	lfbuuiaet	rognib	giamzan	ldwi	nynuf
dangerous		boring			
yscra	lfuaw	texnigci	tique	ghhi	lehorrib

0201

●** ***b)*** *Now describe the picture on p. 7 of your student's book. First, make notes and plan your paragraphs. Use words from a) and words/phrases from the blue box or your own ideas. Write about 80 words in your exercise book.*

in the background/foreground/middle • on the right/left • in front of
high up • glass floor • view • feel free • feel like a bird • see for miles

○ 2 Find and label ▸ *p. 11*

a) *Find and label the following places on the map. Use the back inside cover of your student's book or an atlas:*

The Grand Canyon • Atlanta • New York • Chicago • Las Vegas • Los Angeles

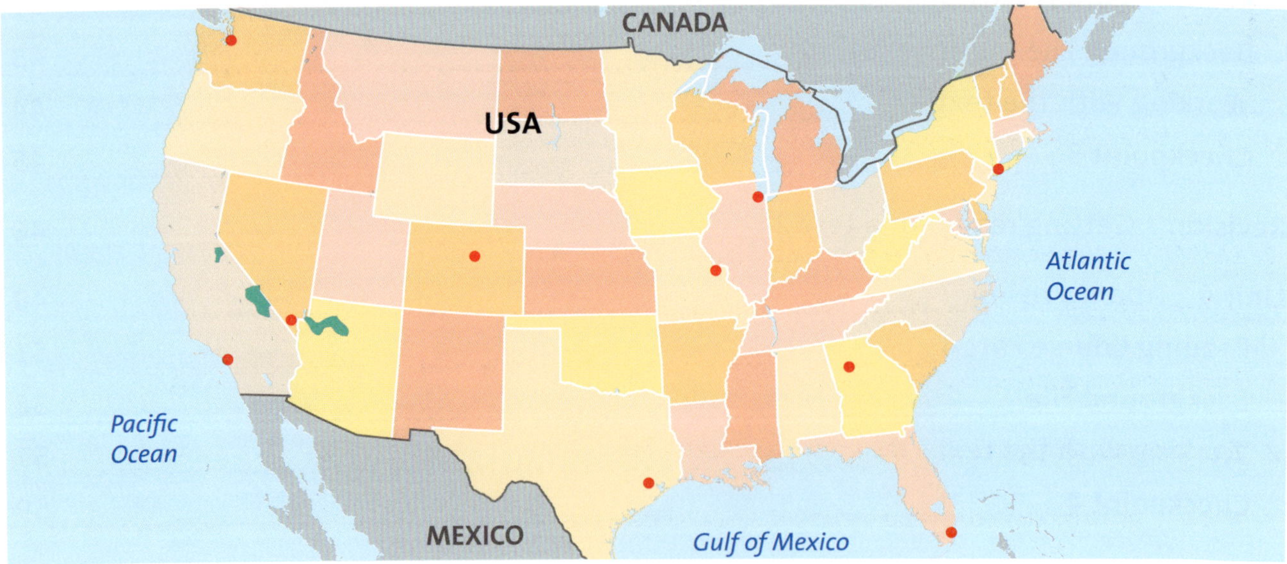

b) *In which US states are the following places? Find and label the states on the map and fill them in the sentences.*

1 The Grand Canyon is in ________________.

2 Las Vegas is in ________________.

3 Hermann is in ________________.

4 Atlanta is in ________________.

5 San Clemente is in ________________.

c) *How many more names of states can you find on pp. 8–11 of your student's book? Label them on the map in a).*

*○ leichte Übung **● schwierige Übung

3 New faces
▸ p. 11

a) Write short profiles[1].

Name: Caitlin ______ ______ ______

Age: ______ ______ ______ ______

Hometown: ______ ______ ______ ______

b) What else do you know about the four students? Tick (✔) the correct box.

		Madison	Jake	Caitlin	Luis
1	Who made the trip to the Grand Canyon by car with his/her father?		✔		
2	Who flew to Las Vegas first?				
3	Who went to the Grand Canyon with a youth group?				
4	Who travelled almost 2,500 miles by car?				
5	Who took Route 66 to the Grand Canyon?				
6	Who rode with a mule train to the bottom of the Canyon?				
7	Who camped at two different places on the rim?				
8	Who did lots of jobs to get enough money for the trip?				
9	Who walked down part of the Kaibab Trail and saw a condor?				

4 WORDS The Grand Canyon puzzle
▸ p. 11

Complete with words from pp. 8–11 of your student's book.

1 The Kaibab is a difficult ... into the Canyon.

2 You can walk along the ... of the Canyon or take a bus.

3 If you ... into the Canyon, wear strong shoes and take lots of water.

4 Madison and her parents stayed at a beautiful ... on the rim.

5 Luis and his friends slept in a ... and cooked their own food.

0304 6 The English word for '*eindrucksvoll, beeindruckend*' is ...

1	_	_	A	_	_
2			r	_	_
3		_	i	_	_
			z		
4		_	o	_	_ _
5	_	_	n	_	
6	_	_	a	_	_

Now you

*Imagine that you're going to visit the Grand Canyon. Write an e-mail to a friend in the US. Tell him/her what you would like to do there. Use words from exercise **4** and write two or three paragraphs in your exercise book.*

[1] profile ['prəʊfaɪl]

5 The Grand Canyon – right or wrong? ▸ p. 11

Test

a) Are the following statements right or wrong? Mark a number.

	Statement	Right	Wrong
1	When you drive from New York to the Grand Canyon, you cross four time zones.	70	75
2	Native Americans once lived in the Grand Canyon.	25	20
3	You are not allowed to camp in the Grand Canyon area.	54	35
4	The Grand Canyon is in the state of Nevada.	30	65
5	The river that goes through the Canyon is the Colorado River.	58	90
6	Las Vegas is in the same state as the Grand Canyon.	15	22
7	You can travel on Route 66 from Chicago to the Canyon.	36	43
8	You can take a mule train into the Canyon.	65	57
9	The job of the rangers is to protect the park and its visitors.	30	25
10	You are not allowed to hike into the Canyon.	65	35

***b)** Add the ten numbers that are marked and write the answer: ______.
The correct answer tells you how long the Grand Canyon is in kilometres. Check your answer in the **Info box**.*

Info box

The Grand Canyon is 446 km long, between 6 and 24 km wide[1] and over 1 km deep[2]. It became a national park in 1919. Over 5 million tourists visit the Grand Canyon every year.

6 Luis's diary ▸ p. 11

Luis wrote a diary about his trip to the Grand Canyon. He used it to write his school essay on p. 9 of your student's book. What do you think Luis wrote in his diary? Write a few sentences for each day.

Day 1: ______

Day 2: ______

Day 3: ______

Day 4: ______

[1] wide [waɪd] *weit* [2] deep [diːp] *tief*

7 STUDY SKILLS Correcting mistakes

▸ p. 11 • SF (p. 147)

Find and mark the grammar and spelling mistakes. There's one in each sentence. Then write what is correct.

	Correct
1 Luis worked hardly to get enough money for his trip to the Grand Canyon.	hard
2 Jake and his dad have begun their journey on August 7.	
3 Madison's parents didn't have much time for a vaccation this year.	
4 On the bus journey Luis and his friends sang songs in spanish.	
5 Caitlins' hometown is New York.	
6 The Park Rangers can give you lots of informations about the Canyon.	
7 Tourists ask often questions about the natural and human history of the Canyon.	
8 Caitlin writes dayly blogs from New York.	
9 The multi-coloured walls of the Canyon look beautifully in the sun.	
10 Jake's dad is a good driver. He drives really good.	
11 Route 66 is the famous highway who goes from Chicago to L.A.	
0507 12 Caitlin and her parents always go in summer to a National Park.	

Now you

Whose journey to the Grand Canyon do you think was the most interesting? Whose journey was the most boring? Why? Write what you think in a few sentences.

8 Extra STUDY SKILLS WRITING Write a blog

▸ p. 11 • SF (pp. 146–147)

Imagine that you went to the Grand Canyon in your summer vacation. Use the information that Caitlin, Luis, Jake and Madison give about the Canyon and write your own blog (for ideas look at Caitlin's blog on p. 8 of your student's book). Write in your exercise book. Remember:

- *brainstorm your ideas*
- *structure your text (beginning, middle, end)*
- *use paragraphs (a new paragraph for a new idea)*
- *structure your information (5 Ws)*
- *make your sentences interesting (linking words, adverbs)*
- *correct your text (grammar, spelling)*

0509

Unit 1 New York, New York

1 New York sights ▸ pp. 12–13

Write the names of the New York sights correctly and match them to the pictures.

6 tteuaS fo ieytbLr | 1 *aaieulnmPtr* | 2 yorklBon gderiB | 3 iaonnwthC | 5 earCnlt karP | 4 pmreEi tteaS iilgunBd

1 the *Planetarium*

2 the ______

3 ______

0601 4 the ______

5 ______

6 the ______

2 Blue box: New York's boroughs ▸ p. 13, p. 172

a) What do you know about New York's five boroughs? Are the statements right or wrong? Mark a letter.

	Right	Wrong
1 Brooklyn is the biggest New York borough.	S	*E*
2 New York's highest buildings are in Manhattan.	L	T
3 Brooklyn Bridge links Brooklyn to Staten Island.	A	L
4 Queens is in the south-west of Long Island.	I	T
5 The Bronx is south of Manhattan.	E	S
6 There's a ferry between Staten Island and Manhattan.	I	M
7 Brooklyn is on Long Island.	S	L
8 Kennedy Airport is in Manhattan.	H	L
9 Brooklyn Bridge is over the Hudson River.	T	A
10 If you run in the New York marathon, you'll run over Brooklyn Bridge.	N	S
11 Manhattan is an island between the Hudson and the East River.	D	N

b) If your answers are correct, the letters give you the name of a famous New York island:

______

3 Blue box: American English (I) ▸ p. 14, p. 170

a) *Which is British English? Which is American English? Find and write pairs.*

~~mobile phone~~	flat	petrol	holiday(s)	(school) year
queue	gas	pavement	downtown	~~cellphone~~
underground	city centre	line	sidewalk	grade
apartment	elevator	vacation	subway	lift

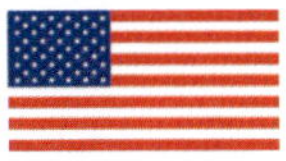

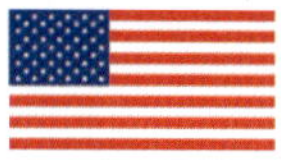

mobile phone – cellphone ______ – ______
______ – ______ ______ – ______
______ – ______ ______ – ______
______ – ______ ______ – ______
______ – ______ ______ – ______

0703

b) *Underline the word in each sentence that is different in American English. Then write the word with AE spelling.*

1 Last year I travelled to New York – by plane, of course. traveled
2 Travelling abroad is exciting! ______
3 Of course I went to a theatre on Broadway. ______
4 I saw my favourite musical, *The Phantom of the Opera*. ______
5 You'd love American ice cream. There are lots of cool flavours. ______
6 Just imagine! The Statue of Liberty is 93 metres high! ______
7 We did a harbour trip too. ______
8 Did you know that Broadway is about 29 kilometres long? ______

4 LISTENING All about ... getting around an American city

▸ p. 14 • SF (p. 148) Track 2

You want to go to the Brooklyn Bridge. Look at the map and listen. Which person gives you the right directions? A, B or C?

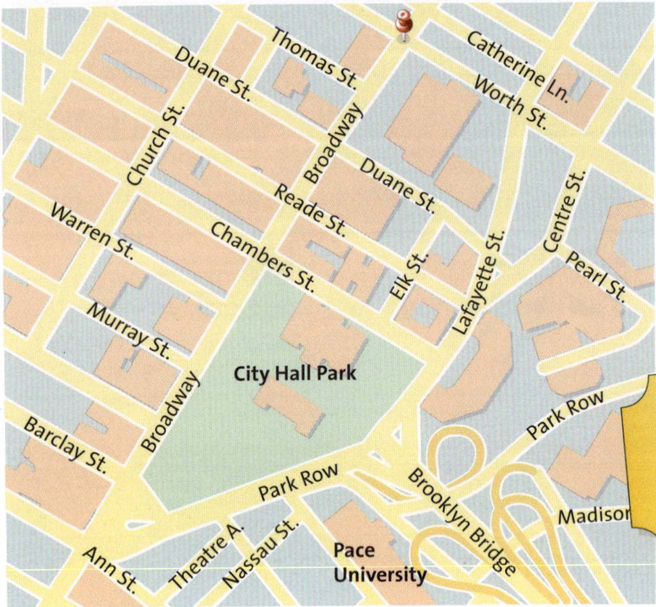

Fun fact

The Brooklyn Bridge is the only bridge where ... a plane could fly over a pedestrian[1] who was walking over a car that was driving over a boat that was sailing over a train. (The subway runs under the East River.)

The person who gives the right directions is ____ .

5 LISTENING Blue box: American English (II)

▸ p. 14, p. 172 Track 3

a) *Different words:*
Are the words you hear British or American English? Write **BE** *or* **AE** *after the number.*

1 AE 4 ______
2 ______ 5 ______
3 ______ 6 ______

b) *Different pronunciation:*
Is the pronunciation you hear British or American English? Write **BE** *or* **AE** *after the number.*

1 ______ 4 ______
2 ______ 5 ______
3 ______ 6 ______

6 WORDS Verbs and nouns that go together

▸ p. 14

Tourists in New York do these things:

a) *Match the verbs to the nouns.*

ask	souvenirs, tickets, a map
buy	a museum, the sights
write	a taxi, the subway, a bus tour
take	postcards
visit	the way, the time

b) *Complete the sentences with words from a).*

1 If you take ______________ , you won't see much.

2 To find the way more easily, you could buy ______________ .

3 If you get lost[2], ask ______________ .

4 Don't forget to ______________ the Guggenheim Museum!

5 Tourists always write ______________ to their families and friends.

[1] pedestrian [pə'destriən] *Fußgänger/in* [2] get lost *sich verlaufen*

7 Talking about New York (Gerund as subject) ▸ p. 15 • GF 1a–b (p. 155)

a) Write the gerunds of these verbs. Be careful with the spelling!

1 plan – *planning*
2 get – ______
3 cycle – ______
4 run – ______
5 shop – ______
6 visit – ______
7 walk – ______
8 write – ______

b) Complete what Ryan and Caitlin say with gerunds from a).

Info box

New York City is often called 'The Big Apple' or 'The city that never sleeps'. With a population of over 8 million it's the biggest city in the USA – the second largest city is Los Angeles. On the streets of New York about 170 languages are spoken.

Ryan *Planning* ______ things to do in New York is fun. I'm really excited. How are we going to get around?

Caitlin Well, ______ around the city is best by bus or subway. ______ everywhere makes you tired and ______ in city traffic isn't healthy.

Ryan But ______ in Central Park is healthy. Can we do that too?

Caitlin Sure, but isn't ______ all the famous sights more important?

Ryan Well, we can do all that first. And ______ at Macy's[1] is important too. I need some presents and postcards for my friends.

0907 *Caitlin* ______ postcards is boring. But I'm sure we'll have enough time for Macy's!

8 He loves being a ... (Gerunds as object) ▸ p. 15 • GF 1a–b (p. 155)

Use a gerund to make one sentence out of two.

1 Caitlin's dad is a New York firefighter. He loves his job.

Caitlin's dad loves being a New York firefighter.

2 Caitlin's dad sometimes gets up in the middle of the night. He doesn't like that.

______

3 Ryan thinks New York is great, but he couldn't live there. He can't imagine it.

______

4 Caitlin often rides her bike in the rain. She enjoys it.

______

5 Ruth often shops at Macy's. She really likes that.

______

6 Visitors to New York always go up the Empire State Building. They love it.

0908 ______

[1] Macy's ['meɪsi:z] *großes Kaufhaus in New York*

9 Liam (Gerunds after prepositions) ► p. 16 • GF 1c (p. 156)

Ryan's cousin Liam in Ireland talks about his time in New York. Use a gerund of the verb in brackets to complete the sentences.

'I was lucky. I had the chance of _going_ (go) to New York on a student exchange. It was great, and now I'm even interested in ______ (get) a job there. I'm fed up with ______ (live) in our village, and I have often dreamt of ______ (move) to another country. I really like the idea of ______ (work) in a big city like New York – and I needn't worry about ______ (not speak) the language. At first I might be a bit scared of ______ (be) alone, but I could visit my exchange family. I'm quite good at ______ (make) friends and I'd have the chance of ______ (meet) lots of new people. I would find out about ______ (join) a sports club or a youth group. I'd never be
1009 tired of ______ (live) in the city that never sleeps.'

10 About you (Mixed gerunds) ► p. 16 • GF 1 (pp. 155–156)

a) *Complete the sentences in the questionnaire with gerunds. Use the ideas in the yellow box or your own ideas.*

1 _Hanging out with friends_ makes me happy.
2 ______ makes me nervous.
3 In my free time I love ______
4 When we're on holiday, I don't like ______
5 At the weekends I really enjoy ______
6 I can't imagine ______
7 Sometimes I'm scared of ______
8 I'm really interested in ______
9 I'm good at ______
1010 10 I'm thinking of ______

- visit museums
- watch horror films
- _hang out with friends_
- read books for school
- live in another country
- go on a student exchange
- get e-mails from friends
- do badly in a test
- buy a new MP3 player
- eat spicy food
- tell jokes
- learn English
- live in a small village/ big city

b) *Choose six words/phrases from the blue box and use them with gerunds. In your exercise book, write three sentences about you and three about your best friend/brother/sister, etc. Use ideas from the yellow box in a) or your own ideas.*

be afraid of • hate • talk about • be tired of • have the chance of • miss • practise • dream of

I often talk about working harder at school, but I usually forget.

11 REVISION WRITING My trip to the ESB

▸ p. 16 • SF (pp. 144, 146–147)

Test

Imagine you went up the Empire State Building in New York. In your exercise book, write a short report about your visit (80–100 words). Read p. 16 of your student's book again for ideas.

Remember the steps of writing:

1 Brainstorming ideas

- collect ideas and put them in order (list, mind map)
- answer the questions Who? What? When? Where? Why? and maybe How? (in a chart)

2 Writing

- structure your text (beginning, middle, end)
- use paragraphs and topic sentences
- write better sentences with adjectives, adverbs, time phrases, linking words, relative clauses

3 Correcting your text

- think carefully about spelling (e.g. take > taking, plan > planned, half > halves)
- check your grammar (tenses, verb endings, irregular verbs, word order)

You can use these phrases if you want:

in the summer holidays • I visited my e-friend • the weather was great, so ... • at the ticket office we ... • my friend told me some ESB facts • we went up in a fast lift • funny feeling in my stomach • when we got to the top, I ... • after that we decided to ... • the ESB is the most exciting building I have ever seen

12 EVERYDAY ENGLISH MEDIATION Where's Times Square?

▸ p. 16 • SF (p. 143)

Test

You are in New York. A young German tourist asks you the way to Times Square, but you don't know so you ask an American woman on the street. Help the tourist.

Info box

Times Square

Times Square got its name from the *New York Times* newspaper building, which stood there in 1904. Today you find bright lights, cinemas, theatres, shops, bars and restaurants there.

You Excuse me, this guy is a tourist and he wants to go to Times Square. I'm a tourist too. So can you help him?

Woman Times Square? That's easy. It's at Broadway and 43rd. He could take the subway. But the bus would be quicker. It's just a few stops.

You Sie sagt, ____________________

Tourist Nein, ich kenne mich nicht aus. Ich gehe lieber zu Fuß. Frag sie bitte, wie weit es ist.

You He says ____________________

Woman OK. You go straight down Broadway, that way. I guess it's 8 or 9 blocks, maybe even 10.

You ____________________

Tourist OK. Und wie lange werde ich zu Fuß brauchen? Ich treffe jemanden in einer halben Stunde.

You ____________________

Woman Yes, that's long enough. He should do it easily. And there's lots to see on the way.

You ____________________

Tourist Thank you und tschüss!

1112

13 WORDS New York puzzle ▸ p. 17

Write the answers in the puzzle and find a famous name for New York.

1 This New York borough has a famous zoo. It's the ... 1

2 New Yorkers often buy food and coffee to go here. 2

3 The name for the place where the towers of the World Trade Center stood is '... Zero'. 3

4 New Yorkers often have this for breakfast. 4

5 The World Trade Center burned and ... on 9/11/2001. 5

6 The 'E' in ESB means ... 6

7 A famous bridge links this borough to Manhattan. 7

1213 8 The bridge in sentence 7 goes over the ... River. 8

Extra Now you

What do you know about 'Ground Zero'? Make notes in your exercise book to prepare a short talk[1] for your English class. Use the information on p. 15 of your student's book and look for more information on the internet.

14 WORDS Talking about jobs ▸ p. 17

a) *Choose from the box and write the correct job names under the pictures.*

actor • artist • caretaker • coach • editor • electrician • engineer • hairdresser • paramedic • photographer • ticket agent • TV presenter • waitress

actor

1214

b) *Would you like to do any of these jobs? Which job do you think is maybe the most interesting? In your exercise book, write what you think and why in about 60 words.*

I think I might like to be a ... I think it's probably the most interesting job because ...

[1] talk [tɔːk] *Rede, Vortrag*

15 REVISION Ruthie's e-mail (if and when) ▸ p. 17

*Ruthie writes this e-mail to an e-friend in the UK. Complete it with **if** or **when**.*

Hi Cathy!

Have to tell you my exciting news! Ryan (my friend's cousin from Ireland) has arrived – and he's just great! He and Caitlin came to meet me at my deli. Ryan loved his first bagel. He said *if* he lived in New York, he would go there all the time. I'm going to join them *when* he and Caitlin go to Times Square later.

My cousin from Texas is coming here soon. I've already made a plan of places to go ________ she's here.

You said you would like to visit New York, so why don't you come in the summer vacation or at Christmas? ______ you came, you could share my room – it's quite big! ______ you came in summer, there would be lots of things to do. ______ you came in winter, we could go Christmas shopping together. ______ I go shopping with my friends – and that's quite often – we usually go to Macy's. It's fantastic. You have to see it too ________ you're here. They've got everything.

Mom always says ______ you wanted a white elephant, Macy's would get it for you!

Write soon,
Ruthie

PS: ______ Ryan asks me out, I'll say YES!

1315

16 EVERYDAY ENGLISH SPEAKING Visiting Liberty ▸ p. 17 Track 4

Test

*It's your first day in New York. Your exchange partner Todd asks you what you would like to do first. You'd like to see the Statue of Liberty. Listen to Todd and give suitable[1] answers or comments in the pauses. Say as much as you can. Use the ideas below or your own ideas. Read the **Fun fact** box first. Do the exercise at least twice.*

1. you want to see everything – the Statue of Liberty first
2. yes, of course – from parents – last birthday
3. read a lot – know some details (see Fun fact)
4. yes – school history lessons – immigration station

Fun fact

The Statue of Liberty

- was born on 28th October 1886
- is 93 m tall
- weighs[2] 204,100 kilos
- her nose is almost 1.5 m long
- her feet are 7.6 m long, so she takes size 879 sandals[3]

You can climb 354 stairs (22 floors) to the crown[4], but since 9/11 it has been closed to visitors.

Just for fun

Why does the Statue of Liberty stand in New York Harbor?
– Because she can't sit down.

[1] suitable ['sju:təbl] *passend, geeignet* [2] weigh [weɪ] *wiegen*
[3] sandal ['sændl] *Sandale* [4] crown [kraʊn] *Krone*

17 READING COURSE Part 1: Visit downtown New York

(Working out the meaning of words) ▸ p. 17 • SF (p. 150)

a) Read this part of a tourist brochure.

Visit downtown New York

Some things have changed, but a lot have remained the same in downtown New York. It's an important center of commerce and has more than 300 years of history.

Downtown has everything: art and museums, architecture, skyscrapers, concert halls, technology, shopping malls, lots of restaurants, entertainment and spectacular waterfront. Don't miss the sunset over the Hudson – it's unforgettable.

There are so many sights to see. The excitement and energy of the city is endless.

You can reach downtown by bus, car or subway. It takes only 20 minutes to walk from the Hudson to the East River. Why not take a luxury ride in a stretch limo?

The food downtown is varied, as New Yorkers will tell you. It is served leisurely or fast. You can eat indoors or out. Or why not dine in elegance?
Get a hot dog from a street vendor or bagels from a deli. And you'll never be bored. There's always lots of fun. Just enjoy the sounds and smells of downtown New York.

So much to see!

b) Now try to understand the underlined words. What can help you to understand the new words? Write them in these four lists:

1 I can understand these words from the **pictures**:

vendor (Straßenverkäufer),

2 These words look like **German** words:

commerce,

3 I can understand these words from the **context**:

changed (verändern),

4 I already know a part of these words or a word from the **word family**:

waterfront (Hafengebiet),

18 Extra Background File ALL STRANGERS ▸ pp. 18–19

a) Read the statements of the five immigrant children on p. 18 of your student's book, then read 1–5 below. Who said what? Write the name.

1 This child felt very small when he/she first saw the building on Ellis Island. It was much bigger than the houses in the town he/she had come from. The child's name was Celia Adler ______.

2 This immigrant said that at first they had lived near the East River in a dark building with lots of other people. This person's name was ______.

3 This child said that everything had been strange to them when they arrived in the US. People had known nothing about the new country they had come to. The child was ______.

4 This immigrant said that they were all strangers, so nobody really felt like a stranger. This child was ______.

5 This immigrant said the weather at sea had been very bad. They were very happy when they sailed into the Bay of New York. This child's name was ______.

b) What do you know about Ellis Island and US immigrants? Tick (✔) the correct answer, A, B or C. Sometimes more than one answer is correct. You need the letters in brackets in c).

1 When was the Ellis Island Immigration Station opened? ☐ A 1892. (S) ☐ B 1900. (I) ☐ C 1924. (H)

2 Why did immigrants want to go to America? ☐ A They were poor and hungry at home. (I) ☐ B For reasons of religion or politics. (S) ☐ C The US paid immigrant workers well. (B)

3 How many immigrants entered the US between 1892 and 1921?
☐ A 4 million. (T) ☐ B More than 12 million. (A) ☐ C 76 million. (S)

4 What is Ellis Island today? ☐ A An immigration station. (L) ☐ B A castle. (P) ☐ C A museum. (U)

5 In the year 2000, how many per cent of the US population were immigrants?
☐ A 13.6%. (B) ☐ B 9.18%. (Y) ☐ C 10.8%. (R)

c) The letters after the correct answers in b) tell you the name of a country where many immigrants came from. Put the letters in the correct order.

The country is ______.

d) Use the information on pp. 18–19 of your student's book and write about 100 words on the topic 'Immigration to the US from 1892 to 1921'. You can use the website www.ellisisland.org to find out more information. Write in your exercise book.

19 WORKING WITH THE TEXT You can tell me ▸ pp. 26–28

a) Read pp. 26–28 of your student's book again, then put the pictures in the correct order. Write numbers.

b) Are the statements right or wrong? Write **R** *or* **W**.

1 Anthony played the guitar on the streets to make money and Kelly sang. R

2 Kelly told Anthony that her mom worked as a nanny for a rich family on Fifth Avenue. ____

3 Anthony and Kelly didn't get much money in the subway. ____

4 They ate their picnic at a place in Central Park called the Ramble. ____

5 Redbeard hit Kelly. ____

6 Kelly asked some people to call the police. ____

7 Kelly wanted Anthony to go home with her. ____

c) Answer the questions in a few sentences. The line numbers will help you.

1 Why does Anthony think he is in a multi-millionaire's apartment? (ll. 34–35)

______

______

2 Kelly doesn't think or act like a 'rich' kid. How do we know this? (ll. 42–53)

______

______

3 Explain Kelly's problem. (ll. 97–119)

______

______

d) What do you learn about the two teenagers in the story? Write a short description of Kelly or Anthony in your exercise book (about 80 words).

3 A trip to Macy's (Simple past or past progressive)

▸ *pp. 30–31 • Revision 7 (p. 64)*

Underline the correct verb form.

Anna, a British exchange student, (stayed/was staying) in New York. Kelly, Anna's exchange partner, (wanted/was wanting) to show her Macy's. Just as they (were crossing/crossed) W 34th Street, Kelly (was saying/said): 'I have to go somewhere for my mom first. I'll meet you in Macy's on the first floor near the elevators in fifteen minutes. OK?'

First, Anna (looked/was looking) at some trendy bags and some funny postcards. Then she (went/was going) to the meeting place. She (was waiting/waited) – 10 minutes, 15 minutes, 20 minutes. But Kelly (didn't arrive/wasn't arriving). What was wrong? Anna (was deciding/decided) to look for Kelly outside. Just as Anna (was walking/walked) down the stairs to the main door, she suddenly (saw/was seeing) Kelly. She (stood/was standing) near the elevators. 'But Kelly! You said the first floor! That's one floor up.'

'No, Anna. **This** is the first floor. You were on the second floor!'

4 STUDY SKILLS Correcting mistakes

▸ *pp. 30–31 • SF (p. 147)*

This is Jürgen's e-mail to a friend in the USA. Mark and correct his mistakes.

	Correct
Hi Todd!	
Last week we have come to Berlin. We visit my grandparents here. On	*came,*
Monday we have seen the Reichstag. It was great. Maybe tomorrow we	
go to the zoo because I enjoy to watch wild animals. We also saw the	
Brandenburg Gate and I made a lot of photos.	
My dad is born in Berlin. When he was a child, lived he in the east part	
of the city. He has told us a lot over the history from the city.	
Just now we sit in a café on the Ku'damm. Dad is takeing photos and	
my sister is shoping. You should visit Berlin too. You'd like it here.	

5 When I'm in a big city, ... (Gerunds)

▸ *pp. 30–31 • GF 1 (pp. 155–156)*

Complete the sentences. Use a gerund and ideas from the box or your own ideas.

When I'm in a big city for the first time, ...

1 I always enjoy *exploring.* ______________________
2 I'm always interested in ______________________
3 I'm sometimes a bit scared of ______________________
4 I love ______________________
5 I hate ______________________
6 I'm always excited about ______________________

- *explore*
- get lost
- look round
- see the sights
- visit museums
- take a bus tour
- see new places
- wait in queues

Unit 2 California, the 'Golden State'?

1 People and places ▸ pp. 34–35

a) Look at p. 34 of your student's book and find words that belong to the following word groups:

People	governor, maid,
Place names	California, beaches,
Adjectives	golden, endless,

2001

b) Use words from a) to make sentences about California. Use as many words from your lists as you can.

1 In California Mexican immigrants often work as

2

3

4

c) When you hear the name 'California', what do you think of? Which pictures (A–H) on p. 34 of your student's book show this best? Write a paragraph in your exercise book.

When I hear the name 'California' I think of sun ... I think picture ...

Info box

The tallest tree in the world is in California's Humboldt State Park. It's 123 m high!

2 WORDS Synonyms ▸ pp. 34–35

a) Match the synonyms.

until	equipment	talk about	awful
mate	woods	terrible	start
gear	till	search for	be quiet
forest	middle	begin	discuss
centre	find	taxi	look for
discover	friend	shut up	cab

2002

b) Where can you use a synonym in the following sentences? Underline the word in each sentence that you can change. Then write the synonym.

1 We talked about the problems of immigrants and minorities in school today. → discussed

2 When did they find gold in California? →

3 In 1848 thousands of people were looking for gold in thc 'Golden State'. →

4 What time does school start in the US? →

5 We talk too much in our English class. The teacher often tells us to shut up. →

3 READING COURSE
Part 2: Where the Gold Rush began (Skimming and scanning) ▸ pp. 34–35 • SF (p. 150)

a) Match the information to the two reading skills.

Skimming

Scanning

- It helps you to find specific information.
- You look at the title, words in bold print, pictures and captions.
- You move your eyes over the text and think of the key words you are looking for.
- You don't read the whole text word for word.
- It helps you to find the main ideas of a text quickly.

b) Skim the text below. Where do you think it's from? Tick (✓) A, B or C.

A From a newspaper. B From a brochure[1] for a state park. C From a school history book.

*c) You have to find some facts about the Gold Rush. Does the text answer important questions? Write Y (Yes) or N (No). Underline the **key words** in the questions below and scan the text.*

1 When did the Gold Rush begin? Y
2 Where is Coloma? ____
3 When did the Gold Rush end? ____
4 Who were the 'forty-niners'? ____
5 Can you still look for gold in Coloma today? ____
6 How do you get to Coloma? ____

VISIT COLOMA, WHERE THE CALIFORNIAN GOLD RUSH BEGAN
The Marshall Gold Discovery State Historic Park, Coloma, California

When, where and how it all began
The Californian Gold Rush began on January 24, 1848, when James Marshall discovered a small piece of gold in Coloma.

The forty-niners
Between 1849 and 1855 over 300,000 men, women and children travelled to California from all over the US, Europe, Australia and Asia. They all wanted to look for gold. They were called 'forty-niners' because most of them came in that year.
Some found gold and became rich. Others went home with nothing.

Coloma now
Today Coloma is a popular state park with thousands of visitors. A statue of James Marshall stands there.

Activities at Coloma
- You can buy a pan[2] in our shop and look for gold in the river.
- You can visit houses from the old days and see how people lived in the 1850s.
- You can discover the history of California's gold towns.
- You can enjoy special events[3] throughout the summer.

How to get there
We are just off Highway 49, about 60 miles north-east of Sacramento.

[1] brochure ['brəʊʃə(r)] *Broschüre* [2] pan [pæn] *Pfanne* [3] event [ɪ'vent] *Veranstaltung*

4 WORDS All about ... growing up in two cultures ▸ p. 36

Complete what Luis's friend Lanh says with words from the box.

advantage • bilingual • cultures • disadvantage • discrimination • ~~ethnic~~ ethnic • experience • fit in • opinion • prejudiced • relations

Hi!

My name is Lanh. I was born in the States, but my family are part of the Vietnamese[1] community here, so we belong to an ethnic minority. For me this isn't a __________ but some Americans are __________ against immigrants like us. Some kids in our school have problems with __________ because they look different and don't speak good English. A boy I know from India once had a bad __________ with some white guys. They said he didn't __________ here and he should go home. In my __________, those guys were just stupid bullies. I think that growing up in two __________ is a big __________. I have American and Vietnamese friends. I speak both languages, so I'm __________ like lots of kids my age. At school my __________ with classmates are good – maybe because I'm good at baseball and because they like my mom's Vietnamese cooking! I wish[2] that all immigrant kids could feel good here, like me.

5 WRITING A help page (Writing an e-mail) ▸ p. 36 • SF (pp. 146–147)

This is part of an e-mail that Rabab, a 14-year-old girl from Pakistan, wrote to a teenage help page. Read about her problems and answer the mail. Help her and tell her what she could do. Write 80–100 words in your exercise book.

...

I've lived in California now for five years, but I still feel lonely at school. The girls in my class always talk together in the break, but never to me. It's because I look different and I'm not interested in things they like – make-up or fashion.

They hang out together after school. They go shopping, and do other stuff. They invite each other to their homes, but they never invite me. They do things that I am not allowed to do, like going to discos and parties. They talk about boys all the time of course, but I have never had a boyfriend. My parents want me to grow up in the culture of our home country. What can I do to find friends at school?

– Rabab K., L.A.

You can use these ideas or your own:

- invite the nicest girl to your home; she'll tell the others about you
- help your classmates with homework in subjects that you're good at
- tell classmates about your home country and why your family came to the US
- join school clubs and sports teams
- if things don't get better, talk to your favourite teacher about your problem

[1] Vietnamese [viˌetnəˈmiːz] *vietnamesisch* [2] wish [wɪʃ] *wünschen*

6 WORDS Californian strawberries ▸ p. 37

Read the text carefully and write the words in the boxes correctly.

Farmers in California grow all kinds of fruit and vegetables because the weather is very warm and sunny. 85% of US strawberries come from California, so strawberry [pnrdcotiuo] *production* is an important [tyudirns] ______. Farmers grow strawberries on huge [lsdiauntri] ______ farms in many areas of the state. From beginning to end strawberry production is a long [spcreso] ______. First workers prepare the ground with big machines. Then they [tnalp] ______ the strawberries and [yspar] ______ the plants with insecticides to kill [tisnecs] ______. Later the workers pick the strawberries and pack them into boxes, ready for the supermarkets.

2306

7 REVISION Verb forms (Past participles) ▸ p. 37

Find the past participles across and down. Then write the three forms of the verbs.

g	r	o	w	n	g	m
s	l	o	s	t	o	a
p	t	f	o	u	n	d
o	a	m	l	u	e	e
k	k	s	d	o	n	e
e	e	s	p	e	n	t
n	n	b	u	i	l	t

grow – grew – grown, ______

______

______

______

______

2307

8 The 'Golden State' (Passive – simple present) ▸ p. 37 • GF 2 (p. 157)

Complete with the simple present passive of verbs from the box.

call • know • make • speak • spend • visit

California *is called* the 'Golden State'. Every year it ______ by millions of tourists from all over the world – and millions of dollars ______ there on its famous sights and attractions. English and Spanish ______ because California is the home of lots of Mexican immigrants. California is also the home of the film industry. The name 'Hollywood' ______ all over the world, just like the films that ______ there.

2308

Info box

With 17 million visitors each year San Francisco is the most popular Californian city. San Francisco is built on 43 hills. It's known as one of the most beautiful cities in the world.

9 What's made where? (Passive – simple present)

► p. 37 • GF 2a–c (p. 157)

Use the information on the map to write passive sentences in the simple present.

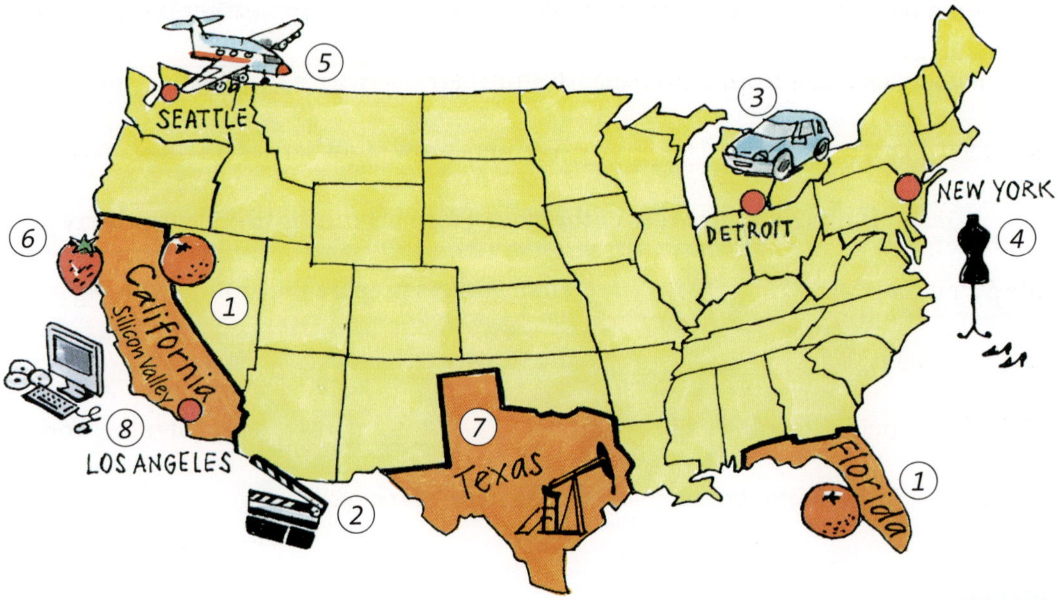

1 grow: *Oranges are grown in Florida and in California.*

2 make: ______

3 produce: ______

4 design: ______

5 build: ______

6 grow: ______

7 produce: ______

8 design: ______

10 When was it done? (Passive – simple past)

► p. 38 • GF 2 (p. 157)

Tick (✓) the correct statements and correct the wrong ones. Choose the right answer from the green box.

1848
1769
Joseph Strauss
Hollywood
Levi Strauss

1 California was discovered in 1910. *Wrong. It was discovered in 1769.*

2 San Francisco was destroyed[1] by an earthquake and fire in 1906. ✓

3 The first jeans were made by Joseph Strauss. ______

4 Gold was first found in 1910. ______

5 The first talking movies were made in Germany. ______

6 Disneyland was opened by Walt Disney in 1955. ______

2410 7 The Golden Gate Bridge was built by Levi Strauss. ______

[1] destroy [dɪˈstrɔɪ] *zerstören*

11 Earthquake country (Passive – simple past) ▸ p. 38 • GF 2a–c (p. 157)

Complete the text and write the simple past passive of the verbs in the yellow box.

Earthquake country: facts

On April 18, 1906 more than 3,000 people ... in an earthquake and the fires which followed. It ... the Great San Francisco Earthquake. On October 17, 1989 San Francisco's Bay Bridge ... and it collapsed. The earthquake lasted[2] only 15 seconds, but 3,300 people ... or ... badly. On January 17, 1994, at 4.31 in the morning, Los Angeles ... by an earthquake which lasted 40 seconds. 72 people died, hundreds of homes ...

2511

kill: *were killed*

call: *was* ______

hit[1]: ______

kill: ______

hurt: ______

hit: ______

destroy: ______

12 Who, where, when? (Passive – simple past) ▸ p. 38 • GF 2a–d (pp. 157–158)

Complete the sentences with the simple past passive. Use **by** *if you need it.*

1

invent[3] – Walt Disney

Mickey Mouse *was invented* by ______.

3

theme park – open

The Universal Studios ______ ______ in 1964.

2

first – make – Levi Strauss

Jeans ______ ______ ______.

4

destroy – earthquake

San Francisco ______ ______ ______ in 1906.

13 Blue box: *any* ▸ p. 38, p. 176

Complete the sentences with **any**, **anyone** *or* **anything**.

1 Maria wanted to hear a bed-time story, but not just *any* story. She wanted the story of how her parents first crossed the US border.

2 When the man took all their money at the border, the Morales were too scared to say ______.

3 Californian fruit farms needed lots of workers, so ______ could get a day job there.

4 When Mrs Morales and her husband arrived in the US, they were glad[4] to get a job – ______ job.

5 Because the Mexican immigrants didn't speak English, they had to do jobs that ______ could do.

[1] hit hier: *treffen* [2] last [lɑːst] *dauern* [3] invent, invented [ɪn'vent] *erfinden* [4] glad [glæd] *froh*

14 WORDS Word building (Prefixes) ▸ p. 38

a) *Add a prefix from the box to make the words negative. If you are unsure, use your Dictionary (pp. 189–219).*

dis- • il- • im- • in- • un-

1 unsafe   4 ____fair   7 ____tolerant
2 ____agree   5 ____appear   8 ____tidy
3 ____possible   6 ____legal   9 ____healthy

Fun fact

In 2000, 55 Oscars were stolen on their way to L.A. to the Award[1] Show. 52 were found next to a garbage bin. Willie Fulgear, the man who found them and gave them to the police, got a reward[2] of $50,000 and two tickets to the show. But a few days later a thief broke into his apartment and stole the money!

b) *Choose words from a) to complete the sentences.*

1 It's ____________ to control[3] the US and Mexican border completely.
2 Most legal and ____________ immigrants from Mexico work on industrial farms or in factories.
3 Some Americans think the state needs immigrant workers, but others ____________.
4 People who don't want immigrants in their country are ____________.
2614 5 Immigrants are often paid badly. It's ____________.

15 SPEAKING Living in California – for or against ▸ p. 38

Test

Would you like to live in California? Think of at least three good things and three bad things. Look at the pictures for ideas, write notes, then prepare your arguments for a class discussion.

Brainstorm your ideas and make notes:

Good things:
good weather – sunny and warm all year;
beaches –

Bad things:
earthquakes; forest fires;

2615

[1] award [ə'wɔːd] *Preis*   [2] reward [rɪ'wɔːd] *Belohnung*   [3] control [kən'trəʊl] *kontrollieren*

16 STUDY SKILLS Interactive listening ▸ p. 38 • SF (p. 148) Tracks 5, 6

Test

Imagine you are in Los Angeles with your family. You call a tour company and listen to a recorded message. To hear information about the tours, you have to press different numbers on your phone.

a) *Listen to Part 1 on your CD (Track 5) and write the correct number.*

1 If you want to find out about the Disneyland tour, press __2__.
2 If you're interested in Beverly Hills and movie stars' homes, press ____.
3 If you'd like to see L.A. from a helicopter, press ____.
4 If you'd like to visit Universal Studios, press ____.
5 If you want to find out about small group tours, press ____.
6 If you want to hear the recorded message again, press ____.

b) *You would like to see where the stars live, so you decide to take the tour that goes to Beverly Hills. Listen to Part 2 (Track 6) and complete the following notes:*

1 The tour leaves ________ daily at ____ and ____ pm.
2 The tour takes ________ hours.
3 The tour buses pick you up from most L.A. ________.
4 The tour costs $ ____ for adults and $ ____ for children under ____.

17 WORDS California words ▸ p. 38

Find group words and put the other words/phrases in the groups. Then complete the sentences below.

immigrants • surfers • people • industries • strawberry production • visit theme parks
film actors • computer companies • go surfing • tourist activities • movie industry
border patrol • ethnic minorities • go hiking in National Parks

1 People	2 I____	3 T____
immigrants,		

1 Silicon Valley is the home of lots of successful ________.
2 ________ is an important industry. 85% of US strawberries come from California.
3 Many of the ________ who work on the strawberry farms are Mexicans.
4 Illegal immigrants from Mexico are often caught by the US ________.

Now you

If you went to California, what would you like to see and do? Write about 100 words in your exercise book.

I think I'd like to see the film studios in L.A. and Hollywood, but I'd like to learn to surf too ...

18 LISTENING A dream that came true

p. 38 • SF (p. 148) Track 7

Test

Luis had to find out some facts about the Golden Gate Bridge for homework, but he made his notes in a hurry and wrote down some wrong details. Listen and correct Luis's mistakes.

1 The bridge is ~~0.7~~ miles long. 1.7
2 It takes about ~~30~~ minutes to walk across the bridge. ______
3 Joseph Strauss's father was ~~an engineer~~. ______
4 Strauss started to build the bridge in ~~1934~~. ______
5 It was opened on ~~June 20th~~ at 12 o'clock midday. ______
6 It cost 25 million dollars to build the bridge. ______
7 It's foggy near the bridge from April to June. ______
8 The bridge is painted gold. ______
9 28 painters work on the bridge. ______
10 Strauss died 10 years after the bridge was finished. ______

19 Extra Alcatraz (Passive – will-future and modals)

p. 39 • GF 2e (p. 158)

Complete the text with these verb forms:

had to be closed • may be taken • should be bought • can be seen • couldn't be done • can be reached • will be remembered

Everybody has heard of Alcatraz or of the gang boss Al Capone, who spent four and a half years of his life there. The prison[1] had to be closed in 1963, but now it's a tourist attraction with lots and lots of visitors. Alcatraz Island ______ from San Francisco, but it ______ by ferry only. Boat tours ______ at any time during[2] the day, but in the summer months tickets ______ ______ at least a week before the tour. Alcatraz ______ by Hollywood films such as *The Rock*. Some prisoners[3] tried to escape from Alcatraz, but it ______.

2819

[1] prison ['prɪzn] *Gefängnis* [2] during ['djʊrɪŋ] *während* [3] prisoner ['prɪznə(r)] *Gefangene/r*

20 Extra Background File WELCOME TO CALIFORNIA! ▸ pp. 40–41

Test

a) What do you know about California? Tick (✓) A, B or C. You need the letters in brackets in b).

1 California is called …

A the Orange State. (S)	B the Yellow State. (A)	C the Golden State. (E)

2 'Silicon Valley' is the home of …

A the movie industry. (E)	B the computer industry. (S)	C fruit and vegetable farming. (A)

3 Hollywood is part of …

A San Francisco. (G)	B San Diego. (E)	C Los Angeles. (N)

4 The first Hollywood movie was made in …

A 1850. (D)	B 1906. (E)	C 1910. (I)

5 You can take a ride on a famous cable car in …

A San Francisco. (Y)	B Los Angeles. (R)	C San Clemente. (T)

6 What are sequoias?

A Mexican food. (N)	B A kind of Californian fruit. (I)	C Big trees. (D)

b) Now write the letters in brackets from a) in the boxes below. If your answers are correct, the letters make a famous Hollywood name. Here are the question numbers:

6	4	2	3	1	5

c) What have you learnt from the information on pp. 40–41? Write two interesting facts about each of these topics:

1 Industry in California 2 Hollywood 3 California's National Parks 4 Earthquake country

1 ____________________

2 ____________________

3 ____________________

4 ____________________

21 WORKING WITH THE TEXT Santa Monica – Episode 1 of a TV series

▸ pp. 49–52

a) Read pp. 49–52 of your student's book again. Which scenes do the pictures show? Write the scene number in the box. Then explain what is happening in the scene.

3

This is the scene where Josh and the others see Jenna with her old car.

She's looking at the engine. Josh is going over to her to help.

This is the last scene.

b) How do you know that Jenna and her family don't have much money?

Jenna needs the job in the café so she's unhappy when she loses it. She

c) Why do you think Josh wants to get to know Jenna?

● *d) Why do you think TV series are so popular[1]? Think about where the action usually takes place (for example, in a hospital, a big company, a hotel, rich and poor families, etc.). Think about problems, relations between characters, feelings. Write about 100 words in your exercise book.*

I think TV series are so popular because they show everyday problems that most people ...

[1] popular ['pɒpjələ(r)] *beliebt*

1 Write the missing words.

1 If you grow up with two languages and speak both, you are ______________.

2 The opposite of 'majority' is ______________.

3 If you go to another country to work and live without papers, you are an ______________ immigrant.

4 The way you think or feel about someone or something is called your ______________.

5 I think being ______________ against immigrants is wrong.

3101 6 What do you think? What's your ______________?

2 Complete the word families.

	Verb	Noun	Adjective
1	experience	______	–
2	produce	______	–
3	–	industry	______
4	______	success	successful
5	discriminate	______	–
6	______	plant	–

3103

3 Complete the sentences with the passive (simple present or simple past).

find • grow
kill • produce

1 Lots of fruit and vegetables ______________ in California.

2 Californian gold ______________ first ______________ in 1848.

3 Computer software ______________ in Silicon Valley.

3102 4 Last year thousands of animals ______________ in Californian forest fires.

4 STUDY SKILLS What's the difference? Complete with skim or scan.

1 If you want to find the main ideas of a text quickly, you should ______________ the text.

2 You have to ______________ the text if you want to find answers to specific questions.

3 You should try to picture key words when you ______________ a text.

3104 4 When you ______________ a text, you look at the bold print, pictures and captions.

20 points

Now you

3105
3106
Write a short essay with the title 'California – a dreamland?' in your exercise book. Write a paragraph each on industry, tourist activities and problems of the state. Use a topic sentence in your paragraphs and your writing skills. (About 100 words.)

Jetzt kann ich ...	**Sehr gut!**	**OK**	**Verbessern!**
HÖREN: Ich kann ...			
... längere Geschichten/Sachtexte verstehen, auch wenn ich einige Wörter nicht kenne.	☐	☐	☐
... aus längeren Listenings Details richtig entnehmen.	☐	☐	☐
... den amerikanischen Akzent heraushören.	☐	☐	☐
... mehrere amerikanische Wörter erkennen und verstehen (z.B. *elevator, gas, cellphone, vacation, sidewalk*).	☐	☐	☐
SPRECHEN: Ich kann ...			
... meine Meinung zu Themen im Englischunterricht frei äußern, auch wenn ich Fehler mache.	☐	☐	☐
... über gelesene Texte sprechen und dazu Stellung nehmen.	☐	☐	☐
... in einer amerikanischen Stadt nach dem Weg fragen.	☐	☐	☐
... in einem amerikanischen *deli* ohne Probleme bestellen.	☐	☐	☐
... über Sehenswürdigkeiten in New York und Kalifornien sprechen.	☐	☐	☐
... über Vor- und Nachteile des Großstadtlebens sprechen.	☐	☐	☐
LESEN: Ich ...			
... weiß, wie ich unbekannte Wörter in einem Text erschließen kann.	☐	☐	☐
... kenne die Lesetechniken *skimming* und *scanning* und kann sie anwenden.	☐	☐	☐
... kann längere Sachtexte und Geschichten lesen und verstehen, auch wenn ich einige Wörter nicht kenne.	☐	☐	☐
SCHREIBEN: Ich ...			
... kenne die Texttypen *diary, essay, presentation, blog, e-mail* und *postcard* und kann sie stilistisch unterscheiden.	☐	☐	☐
... kann die britische und die amerikanische Schreibweise unterscheiden (z.B. BE: *colour, centre*; AE: *color, center*).	☐	☐	☐
... kann Fragen zu Texten der Units 1 und 2 schriftlich beantworten.	☐	☐	☐
... kann meine Sätze mit *adjectives, adverbs, time phrases* und *linking words* verbinden und ausbauen, um sie sprachlich interessanter zu gestalten.	☐	☐	☐
LAND UND LEUTE: Ich ...			
... kenne einige berühmte Sehenswürdigkeiten in New York und Kalifornien (z.B. *the Statue of Liberty, Ellis Island, the Golden Gate Bridge*).	☐	☐	☐
... könnte mich in Manhattan zurechtfinden. Mehrere Straßennamen sind mir geläufig (z.B. *Fifth Avenue, Broadway, 42nd Street*).	☐	☐	☐
... weiß, dass New York fünf Bezirke hat: *Manhattan, Queens, Brooklyn, the Bronx, Staten Island*.	☐	☐	☐
... habe einiges über die Situation von Einwanderern in Kalifornien (*z. B. Mexicans*) gelernt.	☐	☐	☐
... weiß einiges über die Geschichte, Wirtschaft und Industrie in Kalifornien (z.B. Obst- und Weinanbau, Filmindustrie, Tourismus, Computer).	☐	☐	☐

Jetzt kann ich ...	Sehr gut!	OK	Verbessern!
GRAMMATIKVERSTÄNDNIS: Ich kann ...			
... das Gerundium (*gerund*) richtig bilden und als Subjekt/Objekt eines Satzes einsetzen (z.B. *Flying is great. / I love flying.*).	☐	☐	☐
... das Gerundium nach gewissen Verben (z.B. *enjoy, finish, miss, practise*) und nach Präpositionen richtig einsetzen (z.B. *I enjoy reading. / I'm interested in learning languages.*).	☐	☐	☐
... den Unterschied zwischen einem Aktiv- und einem Passivsatz erkennen und das Passiv im *simple present* und im *simple past* richtig bilden. (z.B. *Strawberries are grown in California. / Last year 700,000 tons were produced.*).	☐	☐	☐
... das Passiv mit *by* verwenden, wenn ich den 'Täter' oder 'Verursacher' der Handlung nennen will (z.B. *The Golden Gate Bridge was built by Joseph Strauss.*).	☐	☐	☐
VOKABELVERSTÄNDNIS: Ich kann ...			
... amerikanische Wörter von britischen unterscheiden (z.B. BE: *rubbish, lift*; AE: *garbage, elevator*).	☐	☐	☐
... amerikanische Wörter/Wendungen für eine Wegbeschreibung (z.B. *block, downtown, 34th and Broadway*) richtig verwenden.	☐	☐	☐
... Wörter, die ethnische Minderheiten und ihre Probleme beschreiben, richtig verwenden (z.B. *ethnic minority, discrimination, prejudice*).	☐	☐	☐
SKILLS – LERNEN UND ARBEITEN: Ich ...			
... kenne Arbeitstechniken, die mir helfen, unbekannte Wörter in einem Text ohne Wörterbuch zu erschließen (z.B. Bilder, Überschriften, Kontext, Vor- und Nachsilben).	☐	☐	☐
... kann Lesetechniken wie *skimming* und *scanning* erfolgreich anwenden.	☐	☐	☐
... kann Gesprochenes auf Englisch und Deutsch sinngemäß weitergeben, z.B. bei der Einholung von Informationen (*mediation*).	☐	☐	☐

WAS ICH FÜR MEIN ENGLISCHLERNEN GETAN HABE: Ich habe ...	häufig	manchmal	nie
... im Englischunterricht gut aufgepasst und aktiv mitgearbeitet.	☐	☐	☐
... gelernte Arbeitstechniken bewusst eingesetzt.	☐	☐	☐
... die Aufgaben im Grammar File in meinem Buch bearbeitet.	☐	☐	☐

WIE ICH MICH VERBESSERN KÖNNTE: Ich könnte ...

- ... Vokabel- und Grammatikkenntnisse regelmäßig auffrischen. ☐
- ... häufiger ein deutsch-englisches Wörterbuch verwenden. ☐
- ... ausgewählte Workbook-Übungen der Bände 2 und 3 noch einmal bearbeiten. ☐
- ... mir häufiger amerikanische Texte von meiner CD anhören, um mich an die Aussprache und Betonung zu gewöhnen. ☐
- ... DVDs auf Englisch anschauen. ☐
- ... englischsprachige Zeitschriften oder Websites lesen. ☐

Unit 3 Hermann says 'Willkommen'

1 Hermann and the Schmidts ▸ pp. 54–55

Test

a) What do you know about Hermann, Missouri and the Schmidts? Look at pp. 54–55 of your student's book again. Have you listened to 'Starting a new life' in your student's book? If yes, are the statements right or wrong? Mark a number.

	Right	Wrong
1 St. Louis has an international airport.	15	45
2 The journey by car from St. Louis to Hermann only takes half an hour.	65	35
3 Hermann is on the Missouri River.	74	38
4 Park Street is the main street in Hermann.	36	26
5 There aren't many restaurants in Hermann.	75	90
6 Lots of tourists visit Hermann in summer.	95	44
7 Timo and Anna will go to the same school.	22	30
3401 8 Timo and Jake will go to the same school.	35	22

b) Now add together the numbers that are marked: ________ .

If your answers are correct, you have written the number of students at Hermann High School. Check your answer on p. 55 of your student's book.

c) Look at the photos of Hermann on pp. 54–55. Then write a description of the town in about 60 words.

Hermann is a small town in the state of Missouri. Farmers grow grapes in the area, so outside town

d) Compare Hermann High School (photo F) with your school. Is your school modern too? Has your school got 400 students or more? Has your school got a running track, a football pitch and equipment for athletics? Has your school got a large car park? Write 80–100 words in your exercise book.

Our school is modern too. / Our school isn't as modern as ... Our school looks quite different from ...

2 EVERYDAY ENGLISH WRITING A letter (... to ask for information)

► p. 54 • SF (pp. 146–147)

Test

Imagine that you need information about US schools for a project. Write a letter to Jake Kruger and ask him about schools in Hermann.
*Remember your address and the date. Start and finish your letter correctly. Look at Timo's letter in exercise **2** on p. 62 of your student's book for help.*

Tell him:
- who you are, where you are from
- why you are writing
- where you go to school
- how old you are
- what year you are in

You could ask him about these things:
- the school day
- homework, projects
- school subjects
- clubs
- school holidays

(address) ____________________

____

Dear Jake, (date) ____________________

I'm ____________________

____

____

____

____

____

____

____

____

____

3 WORDS Schools and grades in the USA

► p. 56

a) *Draw lines to match the information in the boxes.*

Ages 6–11	High School	Grades 1–5
Ages 11–14	Elementary School	Grades 9–12
Ages 14–18	Middle School	Grades 6–8

A	below average
B	failure
C	excellent
D	good
F	average

b) *If you went to school in America, what grades would you have in your subjects? Write in your exercise book.*

I think I'd have a B in English, a C in Maths, an A in German and Sport ...

4 WORDS School words: BE and AE ▸ p. 56

a) Write the words in the correct lists.

timetable • *Schulstunde* • vacation • grade • bulletin board • Jahrgangsstufe • *period* • Anschlagtafel • year • schedule • holiday(s) • Ferien • *lesson* • notice board • Stundenplan

Schulstunde	*period*	*lesson*

3604

b) Where are the two students from? The USA or the UK?

I'm in year 9. Our timetable is good this year. I've just read our sports results on the notice board. My next lesson is PE in the gym.

My schedule is OK and my grades aren't too bad, but I'm looking forward to the summer vacation.

Kate is from the ________ .

Josh is from the ________ .

5 EVERYDAY ENGLISH SPEAKING A talk about schools ▸ p. 56

Timo has to tell his new class about school in Germany. He wants to talk about the main differences between US and German schools. Here are his notes:

	Germany	USA
1 grades:	1–6	A–F
2 school day:	not usually afternoon	until 3 pm every day
3 lunch:	usually no lunch	hot lunch at school
4 rooms:	class has own room, teachers come to class	different rooms for different subjects, class has to change rooms between periods
5 vacation:	6 weeks in summer	3 months in summer
6 extracurriculars:	not many	a lot – very important
7 school bus:	not usual	usual

Prepare a three-minute talk from Timo's notes and practise it for class.

German schools are different from US schools in a few ways. For example, school grades are different, the school day and extracurricular activities. First I want to talk about ...

Extra Now you

What do you think is good about American schools? Say why. What do you like better at your German school? Say why. Write two paragraphs in your exercise book.

Some things about American schools are really good. For example, the long summer vacation and ...

6 A sandwich and some milk (Countable/uncountable nouns)

▸ p. 57 • GF 3 (p. 159)

*a) Complete the dialogue with **a/an** or **some**.*

Mom Time to go, Jake. The school bus will be here soon.

Jake OK. I'll just have a sandwich and *some* milk for breakfast if there's ______ white bread. I still have ______ homework to do, but it's just reading.

Mom I thought you had to write ______ Geography essay, and you have ______ work for Science too.

Jake Not for today. I need ______ information for the essay first.

Mom Well, here's ______ money for a hot lunch. And you should take ______ fruit. How about ______ apple or a banana or ______ grapes?

Jake Or how about ______ big piece of chocolate cake?

b) **Extra** *Complete the text with: **some • a • much • many***

Jake hasn't got *much* pocket money, but he would like to have ______ barbecue[1] for Timo and Anna. How ______ kids should he invite? How ______ food should he buy? How ______ money can he spend? Maybe his mom will give him ______ help. He'll need ______ sausages, but how ______ sausages should he buy? And ______ potato salad, but how ______ should he make? He'll need ______ cola, but how ______ bottles can he buy with his pocket money? And very important, he'll need ______ great music and ______ good DJ.

3706

7 WORDS Word building (Nouns from verbs and adjectives)

▸ p. 57

a) Which verb or adjective do these nouns come from? If you are not sure, use your Dictionary in your student's book (pp. 189–219).

activity	– *active*	discrimination	– *discriminate*	discussion	– ______
fitness	– ______	madness	– ______	mediation	– ______
invitation	– ______	nervousness	– ______	weakness	– ______
nationality	– ______	translation	– ______	revision	– ______

b) Now complete the sentences with a noun from a).

1 Timo loves football, so good health and ______ are important to him.

2 There's a Science test next week, so the students have to do some ______ at the weekend.

3707

3 Timo thinks that showing hogs is a very strange ______, but he's going to join the FFA.

[1] barbecue ['ba:bɪkju:] *Grillfest*

8 LISTENING After the Health class

▸ p. 58 • SF (p. 148) Track 8

Test

After the Health class some of the students are talking about food. Listen to what they say, then tick (✓) the correct box.

Who …	Mike	Donna	Dylan
1 enjoyed learning about the food pyramid?		✓	
2 joked about the food pyramid?			
3 likes healthy food best?			
4 gets angry?			
5 thinks chocolate is good for you?			
6 really likes burgers with fries and ketchup?			
7 suddenly feels hungry?			
8 suggests a pizza place?			
9 asks Donna to join them?			
10 suggests a pizza to go?			
11 wants to eat a pizza outside?			
12 is having a party soon?			

Info box

Quick calorie check:	kcal
1 hamburger	254
1 cheeseburger	379
1 serving[1] French fries	294
1 slice[2] pizza Margherita	171
1 can[3] cola (300ml)	200

To burn the calories in one can of cola you have to walk for 23 minutes!

9 WORDS Food

▸ p. 58

a) *Put the food and drink words in the list where they fit best: breakfast, lunch/dinner, snacks*

beans • beef • biscuits • *bread* • carrots • cheese • chicken • chocolate • coffee • cornflakes • crisps • eggs • fish • fruit • fruit juice • hamburgers • ice cream • lamb • marmalade • milk • muesli • nuts • pasta • peas • pork • potatoes • rice • rolls • sausages • soft drinks • soup • steak • tea • toast • turkey • whole-grain products

breakfast	lunch/dinner	snacks

bread, ______	______	______
______	______	______
______	______	______
______	______	______
______	______	______

b) *What's your favourite breakfast? What's your favourite snack? Write in your exercise book.*

My favourite breakfast is cornflakes with milk, then brown bread with cheese or …

[1] serving ['sɜːvɪŋ] *Portion* [2] slice [slaɪs] *Scheibe* [3] can [kæn] *Dose*

10 READING COURSE
Part 3: US students and sport (Finding the main ideas of a text) ▸ p. 58 • SF (p. 151)

a) Read the report carefully. Find and mark the sentences in each paragraph that give you the main idea and the examples or reasons.

(1) US teenagers do not do enough sport to keep fit and healthy. As children grow older, they become less and less active, and by grade 12 physical[1] activity has reached its lowest level[2]. ← **Topic**

(2) Experts agree that students in grades 9–12 spend too much time sitting and spend too little time on physical activities For example, 35% of US high school students do not take part in sports regularly[3]. This fact alone can be the cause[4] of serious health problems when they're adults. ← **Main idea** ← **Example/Reason**

(3) One problem is that our modern lifestyle with its electronic media means that teenagers spend many hours on activities where they just sit. These activities are, for example, watching TV or DVDs, playing video and computer games or using computer and cellphones to contact friends. Studies[5] have shown that 17% of young people in the US watch TV for more than five hours a day.

(4) How students get to school is another cause of physical inactivity[6]. National transportation studies say, for safety reasons most students are taken to school by bus or by car, even if school is only one mile or less away from home. Older students drive to school in their own cars, so walking or cycling to school is something that most high school students just do not do.

(5) What can be done to change the attitude of teenagers to sport and physical activities? In many parts of the USA communities and local[7] government work together to offer physical activity programs for young people. But physical activity is voluntary[8], so students will join programs only if they are motivating, enjoyable, close to home and free.

b) Which of the main ideas below (A–E) goes with which paragraph (1–5)?

A: Physical activity programs of local communities have to be fun. (Paragraph ______)

B: Most high school students do not walk or cycle to school. (Paragraph ______)

C: Our modern lifestyle makes young people physically inactive. (Paragraph ______)

D: US high school students do not spend enough time doing sports. (Paragraph ______)

E: Experts say that students in grades 9–12 sit too much in their free time. (Paragraph ______)

c) **Extra** *What's the general attitude to sports and health in your school year? Do you and your friends take part in physical activities (running, cycling, swimming, etc.) in your free time? Or do you spend more time with electronic media? Write about 80 words in your exercise book.*

[1] physical ['fɪzɪkl] *körperlich* [2] lowest level ['ləʊɪst 'levl] *niedrigstes Niveau*
[3] regular ['regjʊlə(r)] *regelmäßig* [4] cause [kɔːz] *Ursache* [5] studies [stʌdiːz] *Studien*
[6] inactivity [ˌɪnæk'tɪvəti] *Untätigkeit* [7] local ['ləʊkl] *örtlich* [8] voluntary ['vɒləntri] *freiwillig*

11 School is different in Hermann
(The definite article) ▸ p. 58 • GF 4 (p. 160)

*Add **the** where you need it.*

1 Timo thought that ___–___ school in Hermann would be the same as school in Bad Arolsen, but some things are different. ___The___ school that Anna goes to is a middle school.

2 ______ subjects that Timo has in Hermann are not ______ same as the subjects he had in Bad Arolsen.

3 Timo is quite good at ______ homework, but he couldn't do ______ homework he got in Agricultural Science.

4 ______ sports teams in Germany don't have cheerleaders, but ______ sports teams at Hermann High all have cheerleaders.

5 ______ students in Jake's class always go to Maifest and Octoberfest. Tickets for the Festhalle are free

for ______ students.

6 ______ people all over the USA like German sausage, but ______ people of Hermann really love it.

4011 7 On the way to school Jake often listens to ______ music. ______ music he likes best is hip hop.

12 WORDS Facts about Hermann
▸ p. 58 Track 9

Say and write the numbers. Then listen and check.

You see:	You say:
1 Hermann was founded in **1837**.	eighteen thirty-seven
2 Hermann has a population of about **2,674**.	______
3 The town has an area of **6.4 sq km**.	______
4 **54.4%** of the population comes from German families.	______
5 In the 9th grade at Hermann High there are **112** students.	______
6 At Hermann High **52%** of the students are girls.	______
7 In Missouri, summer temperatures can reach **38° C**.	______
8 In winter, temperatures might drop to **– 12° C**.	______

Info box

Missouri …
- became the 24th US state in 1821.
- has borders with eight US states.
- is the birthplace of 33rd US President Harry S. Truman, Jesse James (outlaw[1]) and Mark Twain, author of *Tom Sawyer and The Adventures of Huckleberry Finn.*
- is the home of the world's tallest monument, the Gateway Arch[2] in St. Louis.
- is the birthplace of peanut[3] butter and the ice cream cone[4].

[1] outlaw ['aʊtlɔː] *Bandit* [2] arch [ɑːtʃ] *Bogen* [3] peanut ['piːnʌt] *Erdnuss* [4] cone [kəʊn] *Spitztüte*

13 Blue box: little ('wenig') – few ('wenige')

▸ p. 58, p. 181

a) Underline the right word/phrase in brackets.

1 You should eat very (little/less/few) red meat and butter, and it's a good idea to eat (the least/ less/a few) white bread and pasta too.

2 Jake has to go shopping. In the fridge there's only (a little/a few) milk and (a little/a few) strawberries.

3 Jake is having a snack, (a little/a few) sandwiches and (a little/less/a few) fruit salad.

4 Anna saves (a little/a few) pocket money every week. Timo saves (less/fewer) money than Anna,

4113 but Jake saves (few/the least) money. Jake spends the most and Anna spends (less/a little/the least).

b) Compare yourself with friends/your family. Write sentences with ***a little, less, the least.***

1 How much fast food do you eat? *I eat a little fast food, my* ______

______

2 How much time do you spend on hobbies? ______

______

3 How much money do you save? ______

______

14 What's Anna doing next week? (Present progressive, future meaning)

▸ p. 59 • GF 5c (p. 161)

This is what Anna is doing next week. Read her notes and complete the text with the present progressive.

Mon	start Geography project
Tue	buy present for Jake with Timo
Wed	3 pm – jazzdance class
Thu	after school: shop in town with mom
Fri	Kelly and Sue come to visit for the first time
Sat	Jake's party
Sun	visit St. Louis with the Krugers

Just for fun

What are you doing tomorrow?
– Er... Oh, I know!
Yesterday's homework.

On Monday Anna *is starting* her Geography project. After school on Tuesday Anna and Timo ______ a present for Jake. On Wednesday at 3 pm Anna ______ to a jazzdance class. On Thursday after school she ______ in town with her mom. On Friday Kelly and Sue ______ to visit for the first time. On Saturday Anna ______ to Jake's

4114 party. On Sunday the Schmidts ______ St. Louis with the Krugers.

Now you

What are you doing 1) after school today 2) next Tuesday 3) next weekend? Write two sentences each in your exercise book.

After school today I'm going to town with two friends. We're meeting two other friends there and ...

15 STUDY SKILLS Summary writing: Hermann Maifest ▸ *p. 59 • SF (p. 145)*

Test

a) Read the story about Dylan and his friends at Maifest in Hermann.

It was the third weekend in May, Maifest time. The whole of Hermann was excited. The town was alive with attractions, shows, singing and dancing.

'Now be sure to have a good time, you guys, and take care[1] of Bobby, Dylan. Don't lose him. There will be so many visitors in town this weekend,' said Mrs Kaiser, as Dylan, Donna and Mike left for the Maifest. The three students were part of the High School Band, so they were already dressed in their German costumes[2]. Dylan even had a solo part on his trumpet. Nobody could play the trumpet like Dylan.

'I just love Maifest', Donna said as they walked through the busy streets in the sunshine. 'Why can't we have Maifest every weekend? There's so much to see, and lots of cute[3] guys come from other high schools!'

'Girls!' said Dylan, as they turned into Schiller Street. They stopped to listen to the Spitzbaum German Band, then they looked at the food stalls[4] and the big market at Volksplatz. Bobby loved the puppet[5] show and the mini train ride. Then they met more friends, laughed and joked and cheered.

An hour later Dylan looked at his watch. It would soon be time to go to the Festhalle for their concert. 'I have to take Bobby home first, then I'll meet you guys in the Festhalle, OK? Come on, Bobby, we have to go home now. Bobby? Bobby? Where is he? Where's Bobby?' Bobby wasn't there ...

Dylan, Donna and the others looked everywhere, but Bobby was nowhere. They asked lots of people on the streets, but nobody had seen him. Maifest was no fun any more. Dylan was scared, really scared. Had someone taken his little brother?

'Dylan, I think you should call your mom,' said Donna in a nervous voice.
'But Mom will kill me, Donna. She told me to look after Bobby – but I didn't. I was just too busy having fun with you guys. And what about our concert? I have to play my trumpet solo in ten minutes! Bobby must be somewhere. We just have to look everywhere again – fast.'

'Hey, look! Here comes the parade[6]! Look at the costumes! It's just like the very first Maifest in the 1870s,' said Mike, but nobody was listening ...

'Call your mom, Dylan. You have to call her,' said Donna again. Nervously, Dylan took his cellphone out of his pocket ...

'Hey, guys, look at the old German cars in the parade, and the old fire truck[7] and ... Dylan, look who's sitting in the old fire truck with my dad, wearing a fire helmet – it's Bobby!'

'Oh, Mom! Hi, Mom! Er ... it's Dylan. I just wanted to tell you that we're having a great time – Bobby too.'

b) Mark the sentences which tell you the main events or important facts. Then write notes in your exercise book.

c) In your exercise book, write a summary of the story in your own words. Remember to leave out direct speech, details and description, and use the simple present.

The story is about Dylan, a student from Hermann High School, who goes to Maifest with his friends and his little brother. First they ...

[1] take care [keə] *aufpassen* [2] costume ['kɒsthuːm] [3] cute [kjuːt] *süß, hübsch* [4] stall [stɔːl] *Stand, Bude* [5] puppet ['pʌpɪt] *Marionette, Puppe* [6] parade [pə'reɪd] [7] fire truck [trʌk] *Feuerwehrauto*

16 Extra Background File GOING WEST ▸ pp. 60–61

a) Read the statements. Are they right or wrong? Mark a letter.

	Right	Wrong
1 Hermann was founded in 1837.	I	S
2 When World War I started, the people of Hermann stopped speaking German.	N	T
3 The first states of the United States were in the West.	L	D
4 Missouri became a state in 1840.	O	E
5 After 1848 Missouri became the 'Gateway to the West'.	P	I
6 Wagon trains were the safest way to travel to the West.	E	C
7 People bought all the things they needed for the long journey in Hermann.	B	N
8 More than half a million people travelled west with the wagon trains.	D	P
9 The first railway across the country was finished in 1869.	E	A
10 About ten per cent were killed by wild animals or Native Americans.	S	N
11 A few Native Americans died from illnesses the European settlers brought.	R	C
12 Today only 1.5% of the US population are Native Americans.	E	T

If your answers are correct, the letters give you the name of a town in Missouri: ______________________

b) Answer the questions in one or two sentences each.

1 **A:** Why was the town of Hermann founded?

____

____

____

2 **B:** Why did so many people want to go west in the years after 1848? Write two reasons.

____

____

____

3 **C:** Why was the journey west so hard?

____

____

____

4 **D:** What happened to the Native Americans when the settlers went west?

____

____

____

17 WORKING WITH THE TEXT Angus Bethune's moment ▸ pp. 68–70

a) Finish the statements with information from the story.

1 The story is about a boy called Angus who *has problems at school because he's big.*

2 Angus is elected Winter Ball King, but ______

3 Angus was elected because Melissa's boyfriend, Rick, ______

4 Angus is OK on the dance floor because ______

5 Melissa tells Angus that ______

6 After the first dance ______

7 When Angus and Melissa dance the second time, ______

8 At the end Rick is angry and ______

9 But Angus is happy because ______

b) Choose a picture and describe what is happening. Write in your exercise book.

1

2

3

I think Picture 1/2/3 shows the scene where ...

c) Do you like the ending? Why or why not? Ideas:

funny · fantastic · surprising · clever · unrealistic · sad · silly

In my opinion ______

______

______

d) What do you think is more important?

- *looking good and acting cool (like Rick)*
- *being a really nice person (like Angus)*

What are the advantages and disadvantages of both? Write about 80 words in your exercise book.

1 Write the missing words.

1 Bad Arolsen is the German ______________________ of Hermann, Missouri.

2 Farmers in Hermann grow grapes to make ____________________.

3 Timo now has a new school subject called American ____________________________.

4 Jake: 'Being in the FFA will look good when I ______________________ college or my first job.'

5 US school grade C means ______________________.

4501 6 American girl students like to become ____________________ for their school's sports teams.

2 Put in a/an, some, much or many.

1 Timo hasn't got ____________ homework today, but he needs ______________ information about Hermann's wineries for ______________ essay.

4502 2 He hasn't found ________________ facts in his school books, but there's still ______________ time to ask questions at the wineries.

3 Add the where you need it.

1 Jake: I need some money for the weekend. I'm visiting a friend in St. Louis. The problem is, I've already spent ____________ money I got for my birthday.

Timo: I know what you mean. _______ money is only a problem when you don't have any.

2 _______ tourists always come to Hermann at Maifest and Octoberfest time. Lots of them are from

4503 Germany. __________ tourists who took part in the Maifest parade were from Rüdesheim.

4 STUDY SKILLS
Summary writing: Find and tick (✓) the five correct statements.

To write a good summary you should …

- give only the most important information from the original text. _____
- tell the reader what the text or story is about in the first few sentences. _____
- explain **who** does **what**, **where**, **when** and **why**. _____
- 4504 leave out examples and direct speech. _____
- give lots of details. _____
- use the simple present and your own words. ____
- use lots of adjectives for description and comparisons. _____

20 points

Now you

4505 4506 *Write a short essay with the title 'US and German schools: a comparison'. Use the information in your student's book and exercise **5** of this unit in your workbook. Remember your writing skills. Write about 120 words in your exercise book.*

Here are some exercises that will help you with your practice test 2.

1 WORDS Holiday words ▸ pp. 72–73

a) Match the words in the box to the kind of holiday. Make three lists.

art galleries • *ball games* • bay • *cabin* • camping gear • caravan • castle • cathedral • church • column • cows • downtown • hike • lake • market • mosque • museum • ocean • palace • parliament • path • rocks • sea • sunglasses • surfboard • swimming trunks • swimsuit • tent • ticket office • tour guide • towel • tower • trail • valley • views • visibility • volleyball • walking shoes

A mountain holiday: *cabin,* ______________________________

____

A beach holiday: *ball games,* ______________________________

____

A sightseeing holiday: *art galleries,* ______________________________

____

b) Which kind of holiday from a) do you like best? Write your reasons in a paragraph.

I like sightseeing holidays best because ...

____

____

____

____

2 Going on holiday (Mixed prepositions) ▸ pp. 72–73

Complete the sentences with the correct prepositions: in • of • to • at • on • by

1 We usually go *on* holiday ______ summer.

2 When you flew ______ New York, did you land ______ JFK? It's ______ Queens, isn't it?

3 When it's 10 o'clock ______ the morning in New York, it's 4 o'clock ______ the afternoon in Germany.

4 I've taken a really good photo ______ the Golden Gate Bridge. I'll show it ______ you tomorrow.

5 My dad doesn't like flying. He goes everywhere ______ train or car.

6 My mum doesn't like sitting ______ a beach all day. She likes going ______ boat trips or bus tours.

3 My dream holiday (Conditional sentences 2) ▸ pp. 72–73 • Revision 11 (p. 65)

Where would you spend your US dream holiday – if you could?
Grand Canyon, New York, San Francisco, Las Vegas, Los Angeles, Miami, Washington? Choose a place.
If you **went** *there, what* **would/could** *you* **do**? *Write a paragraph and use at least two conditional 2 sentences.*

I would spend my US dream holiday in ... if I could. I would go to ... If I went there, I could ...

____

____

____

____

____

4 SPEAKING Making suggestions, agreeing or disagreeing ▸ pp. 72–73

a) *How would you make a suggestion? How would you agree or disagree with a suggestion? Match.*

- Making suggestions
- Agreeing
- Disagreeing

- Yes, let's do that.
- We could go/watch ...
- I'm not sure I like that idea.
- That's a good/great ... idea.
- What about going/watching ... ?
- I don't really want to do that.
- Let's go/watch/...

b) *Look at the photos of the beach and the aqua park. A friend suggests going to one of these places. What would you say? Write a dialogue in your exercise book.*

Unit 4 Atlanta rising

1 Atlanta, Georgia ▸ pp. 76–77

a) Look at pp. 76–77 of your student's book and listen to 'An Atlanta timeline', also in your student's book. Are the statements below right or wrong? Mark a letter.

	Right	Wrong
1 Atlanta is the capital of Alabama.	A	O
2 Atlanta was founded in 1847.	B	R
3 Black slaves from Africa worked on the cotton plantations in the South.	C	K
4 The American Civil War began in 1865.	A	L
5 In 1864 Atlanta was burned down.	L	E
6 The Southern states won the Civil War.	S	N
7 The chemist John Pemberton made a drink which is known all over the world.	N	S
8 Martin Luther King was a Civil Rights leader.	I	A
9 CNN, the world's first 24-hour news station, started in Atlanta in 1980.	T	P
10 Shirley Franklin was elected Atlanta's first black woman mayor in 1999.	O	L
4801 11 Today 61% of Atlanta's population is black.	I	S

b) Put the letters you have marked in the correct order to make the name of the man who opened the Atlanta Olympic Games:

____

c) What do you remember about the events on the Atlanta timeline from 1968–2002? In your exercise book, describe each event in one or two sentences.

In 1968 the Civil Rights leader Dr Martin Luther King was killed. In 1980 ...

2 Blue box: German 'während' ▸ pp. 76–77, p. 185

*Complete the sentences with **during** or **while**.*

1 Before the American Civil War white plantation owners got rich *while* their black slaves had a terrible life.

2 ______________ the Civil War Atlanta was burned down.

3 Over 620,000 Americans were killed ______________ the years 1861 to 1864.

4 In 1884, ______________ Pemberton was trying to help people feel better, he made a world-famous drink.

5 Martin Luther King led[1] the non-violent Civil Rights Movement, ______________ others wanted to fight violence with violence.

4802 6 ______________ the years 1955 to 1968 King worked very hard for the rights of African Americans.

Fun fact

Georgia is the USA's top producer of the '3 Ps' – peanuts[2], pecans[3] and peaches[4].

[1] lead, led, led [li:d] *führen* [2] peanut ['pi:nʌt] *Erdnuss* [3] pecan [AE: pɪ'kɑ:n] *Pekannuss* [4] peach [pi:tʃ] *Pfirsich*

3 WORDS All about ... television ▸ p. 78

a) Match the words and the definitions.

1 news
2 documentary
3 TV listings
4 prime time
5 viewer
6 contestant
4903 7 rerun/repeat

- a programme which gives information about events or topics
- a person who watches television
- a programme that is shown on TV for a second or third time
- a person who takes part in a game show or competition
- a programme that reports true events of the day
- information about names and times of TV programmes for the week
- the time when most people watch TV in the evening

b) Now explain these words.

1 A TV host is someone __________

2 A comedy is a __________

3 A comedian __________

4 A crime series __________

4 EVERYDAY ENGLISH SPEAKING Talking about soap operas ▸ p. 78 Track 10

Test

*Listen to the dialogue between Katie and her brother Mason. They have different opinions about TV soap operas. What do you think? Do you agree with Katie or with Mason? Make notes and prepare your arguments **for** or **against** soap operas for a two-minute talk in class. The words and phrases below will help you.*

I (don't) agree with ... • In my opinion • My view is that ... • I think ... • From my point of view ...
modern • fantastic • awesome • cool • interesting • terrible • stupid
silly • boring • unrealistic

NOTES: For/Against soap operas

Katie's arguments:

Mason's arguments:

Your opinion:

4904

5 EVERYDAY ENGLISH WRITING

My favourite TV programme

▸ p. 78 • SF (pp. 146–147)

Test

Write an e-mail to a friend about your favourite TV programme (show, series, etc.). First make notes which answer these questions:

- When is it on (day and time)?
- How often is it on?
- Which channel is it on?
- What kind of programme is it (music programme, crime series, soap opera, etc.)?
- Who is in it (presenter, actors, etc.)?
- If there's a story, what is it about?
- Why do you like the programme?

Write the e-mail in your exercise book. The ideas in the box will help you:

Dear ...

My favourite programme was on TV again yesterday/last night.

I must tell you about it! It's called ... and it's on at ... pm

every ... It's on channel ... and it lasts for ... It's about ...

It's really interesting/exciting/scary ...

It's my favourite programme because ...

6 MEDIATION TV in the USA

▸ p. 79 • SF (p. 143) Track 11

Test

Brad, a boy from Atlanta, is staying with your neighbours, the Bergers. Brad doesn't speak much German and your neighbours don't speak much English. They ask you to mediate.

Mrs B. Kannst du Brad fragen, wie er deutsches Fernsehen findet?

You *Mrs Berger wants to know what you think of German TV.*

Brad Well, my problem is that I don't understand much. But I think it's funny when American actors suddenly speak German. Yesterday I watched the Simpsons and Bart Simpson was speaking German. I don't know what he was saying, but just listening to him was real funny.

You ...

Listen to the rest of the conversation and mediate for the family and Brad. Remember, just give the most important information.

Info box

Atlanta is ...

- the fastest growing city in the USA.
- one of the cleanest cities in the USA.
- maybe the 'greenest' city in the USA because of the green oak trees[1] that line[2] its streets.

Atlanta has ...

- the world's largest aquarium, opened in 2005.
- the world's busiest international airport with over 77 million passengers[3] a year.
- 32 streets with the name 'Peachtree'.
- 41 golf courses.
- 54 parks.

[1] oak tree ['əʊk tri:] *Eiche* [2] line [laɪn] *säumen* [3] passenger ['pæsɪndʒə(r)] *Passagier*

7 READING COURSE
Part 4: Summer jobs in the US (Drawing conclusions) ▸ p. 79 • SF (p. 151)

a) Read the magazine article carefully to understand the main facts.

When summer comes, for most teens it means lots of free time, in the US usually from June to August. Some students go to summer camps or go on vacation with family. The ones who stay at home often take part in organized sports programmes or just hang out with friends. But many teens need money, for their families and for themselves, so they try to organize a job for the summer vacation. (1)

What kind of summer vacation jobs do teens do?
Younger teens look for jobs in their hometowns. About 25% have jobs in restaurants, about 25% help out in shops, 11% have an office job. The rest do garden work or work for a pizza service. Some work at petrol stations and wash cars. (2)

We looked at statistics and found that now there are not as many summer jobs for teen workers as in past years. Why is this? We spoke to high school students in three US states. Here are some of their comments: Matt B., 16, from Germantown, Tennessee said: 'I have a part-time job in a supermarket during the school year and I'm looking for a summer job too. I want to work because I need the money for college later. The problem is that there aren't many jobs for teens. Adults who have lost their jobs and old people who need money are also looking for low-paid[1] work, so they get the jobs.' (3)

15-year-old Carol S. from San José, California said: 'There are lots of summer jobs here because of all the tourists. My sister is 18. She has work experience and she's at university, so she can work for longer than three months in summer. She has no problem getting a job, but it's more difficult for me.' (4)

'A lot of kids in my grade apply for a summer workplace, but mostly without success. Kids our age only get boring jobs and not much money. Some employers[2] think that older people work harder and better. Some have the view that teenagers want money but don't really want to work for it. But we have to start somewhere. We need early work experience,' said 15-year-old Guy C. from Missouri City, Texas, 'but sometimes it's hard to get.' (5)

b) In which paragraphs does the text give direct information about the following?

- how much summer vacation high school students have: Paragraph(s) ______
- how high school students spend the summer vacation: Paragraph(s) ______
- what kind of work high school students do: Paragraph(s) ______

c) The text says that now there are not as many summer jobs for high school students as in the past. Why is this? No direct reasons are given. Find at least two facts in the text which explain the reasons indirectly, and draw a conclusion about the reasons. Write the line number(s).

Jobs that high school students could do are given to adults without work and to

____

____

____

d) **Extra** *If you were a high school student in the US, would you try to get a summer vacation job? What kind of work would you like to do? Write a paragraph in your exercise book.*

[1] low-paid [ləʊ] *schlecht bezahlt* [2] employer [ɪm'plɔɪə(r)] *Arbeitgeber*

8 WORDS Word building (-able) ▸ p. 79

a) Match the adjectives to their meanings.

- enjoyable
- eatable
- readable
- usable
- unthinkable
- returnable
- unpronounceable
- washable

- good enough to eat
- you can enjoy it
- easy, interesting to read
- you can return it
- good enough to use
- you can wash it without problems
- impossible to imagine, too bad to think about
- too difficult to pronounce

b) Now choose adjectives from a) to complete the sentences.

1 Madison says we would have a very ____________ holiday in Atlanta.

2 My MP3 player is old but it's still ____________.

3 I have an English friend who's learning German. He thinks some German words are ____________.

4 I think I've lost my cellphone. That would be ____________!

5 You'll enjoy Katie Smith's new book. It's very ____________.

5208 6 That hamburger is still in the fridge. Yuck! I don't think it's ____________ any more.

9 I've known her for four years (Present perfect with 'for') ▸ p. 79 • GF 6a (p. 162)

Answer the questions. Use the present perfect and **for**.

1 Is Madison your friend?
– Sag ja, du kennst sie seit vier Jahren.
Yes, she is. I have known her for four years.

2 Has Madison got a new computer?
– Sag ja, sie hat ihn seit zwei Wochen.
Yes, she has. She ____________

3 Does Madison's mom work for CNN?
– Sag ja, sie arbeitet dort seit drei Jahren.
____

4 Is Madison in a school sports team?
– Sag ja, sie ist in der Basketball-Mannschaft seit sechs Monaten.
____

5 Does Madison want to take part in TYCTWD?
– Sag ja. Sie will seit einem Jahr ihre Mutter bei der Arbeit besuchen.
____

10 How long has she worked for CNN? (Present perfect with 'for')

▸ p. 79 • GF 6a (p. 162)

*Ask questions with **How long** ... about the statements. Then write answers with the information in brackets and **for**.*

1 Madison's mom works for CNN. (about three years)

How long has she worked for CNN? – She has worked there for about three years.

2 Madison is at the Martin Luther King High School. (one year)

____

3 Madison and her mom are in the traffic jam. (20 minutes)

____

4 The traffic downtown is bad. (three months)

5310 ____

11 Blue box: German 'seit'

▸ p. 80, p. 186

*A local reporter is asking tourists some questions about their stay in Atlanta. His first question is: 'How long have you been in Atlanta?' Complete what the tourists say with **since** or **for**.*

1 
We've been here *since* yesterday.

4 
______ last Sunday. I'm visiting friends.

2 
______ my birthday last week.

5 
I've been here ______ a week now. It's a great city.

3 
______ about five days now.

6 
I've been here ______ ten years – I live here!

5311

Now you

*How long have you done these things? In your exercise book, write a sentence each with **since** and **for**.*

1 How long have you lived in your village, town or city?
2 How long have you been in your school class?
3 How long have you known your English teacher?
4 How long have you had your pet, MP3 player or computer?

I've/We've lived in our town for about six years. Or: *I've/We've lived in our town since 2004.*

12 REVISION WORDS Jobs and people

▸ p. 80

a) What's the word for somebody who ...

1 puts out fires? firefighter

2 goes to live and work in another country? __________

3 doesn't eat meat? __________

4 is the most important person in a US state government? __________

5 lives in the US but comes from a Spanish-speaking country? __________

6 watches TV? __________

7 looks after your teeth? __________

8 gets money for making people laugh? __________

9 interviews people and reports news __________

10 is the leader of a town government? __________

11 shows tourists round famous cities and sights and gives them information? __________

5412 12 sells tickets for concerts, tours, etc.? __________

b) Write the names of at least ten jobs. Use the Dictionary in your student's book (pp. 189–219) for help.

____

____

____

13 LISTENING Malcolm X

▸ p. 81 • SF (p. 148) Track 12

Test

Listen to the information about Malcolm X and complete the text.

Malcolm X was born in Nebraska in the year __________. His real name was Malcolm __________. Like Martin Luther King he first became a __________, then a black speaker and civil rights leader. But he __________ with King that non-violent protest was the only way. Black people wanted __________, and many thought that it was coming too slowly. Malcolm X believed that blacks should fight for equal[1] __________ not with words, but with violent __________. He said that white racists[2] only spoke the language of __________, not the language of peace[3]. Many young blacks followed him. There were riots[4] in the big cities of America and many people were killed. Malcolm X was killed in 1965, while he was giving a __________ in __________.

[1] equal ['i:kwəl] *gleich* [2] racist ['reɪsɪst] *Rassist/in* [3] peace [pi:s] *Frieden*
[4] riot ['raɪət] *Ausschreitung, Aufruhr*

14 REVISION WORDS Opposites

▸ p. 81

a) Find and write pairs of opposites.

cloudy • success • smart • soft • fantastic
dead • leave • minority • a little • pick up
advantage • better • life • weak • easy

hard • disadvantage • failure • a lot • drop off
death • strong • alive • stupid • return
cloudless • majority • worse • difficult • awful

cloudy	–	cloudless		–			–
success	–			–			–
	–			–			–
	–			–			–
	–			–			–

5514

b) Write four sentences. Use a pair of opposites from a) in each sentence.

1 My brother thinks game shows are fantastic, but my dad thinks they're awful.

2

3

4

5

15 STUDY SKILLS Research

▸ p. 81 • SF (p. 141)

a) What is important when you do research? Write Y (Yes) or N (No) next to the statements.

1 use only Wikipedia N
2 use only one good source
3 use more than one source
4 try to use at least one English source
5 take notes in your own words
6 always take notes in your own language
7 always use full sentences for your notes
8 look for answers to the 5 Ws (Who, What, When, Where, Why + How)
9 copy whole sentences from your sources
10 use only key words for internet search engines

b) Now use the information in a) to find out about the African-American Muhammad Ali (Cassius Clay), and his role in the US Civil Rights Movement. Write a short text (about 100 words) with the most important information in your exercise book:

Who was Muhammad Ali? Why was he so popular? Why was he in prison[1]?

[1] prison ['prɪzn] *Gefängnis*

16 Extra Background File Towards the African-American dream ► pp. 82–83

a) Read pp. 82–83 of your student's book again and complete the information below.

1 In 2006, 12.4% ______ of the US population were black.

2 In 2005, ______ of the black students left school without finishing.

3 The average black family had about $ ______ less to spend per year than the average white family.

4 Statistics say that in 2006 there were about ______ times more poor black people than poor white people.

5 In 2006, ______ of the people in prison were black.

6 The first black players joined the NBA in ______ .

7 Today you can't imagine ______ without black players.

8 In 2009 Barack Obama became the first African-American ______ .

b) Write three sentences about African-American musicians. Use your own words.

______

______

______

______

c) Answer the questions about the Rodney King riots.

1 Where and when did the Rodney King riots take place? ______

______

2 Who was Rodney King and what happened to him? ______

______

______

3 How do we know what exactly happened to Rodney King in the attack? ______

______

4 What happened to the policemen? ______

5 Why were there terrible riots in Los Angeles? ______

______

______

d) From what you have read, do you think that today black Americans have the same chances as white Americans? Think of the areas: education, income, politics, sports, music. Write a paragraph (80–100 words) in your exercise book.

17 WORKING WITH THE TEXT Melba's story ▸ pp. 91–94

a) Read p. 91 of your student's book again. Are the statements right or wrong? Write R or W.

1 After slavery ended, black people were segregated from white people for about a hundred years. R

2 There were separate schools for white children and for black children. ______

3 Only schools were segregated. ______

4 Schools for black children were just as good as schools for white children. ______

5 All states wanted to keep the new law against segregation in schools. ______

b) Now read the story about Melba on pp. 92–94. Say in one sentence what these people did.

1 The ticket man didn't let Melba ride on the merry-go-round and called her 'nigger'.

2 The Supreme Court ______

3 A teacher at Melba's black school ______

4 The white students at Central High School ______

5 A white Californian family ______

c) Go through the text on pp. 92–94 in your student's book again and write notes about the brave things Melba did.

NOTES

d) Do you think Melba was a hero? Use your notes from c) and write a short essay in about 100 words. Write in your exercise book.

18 My book quiz

▸ p. 94

a) How well do you know your student's book? Match the information about the four students to the pictures. Check your answers in your book.

- has a visitor from Ireland
- has a little sister called Maria
- has a friend called Ruth
- goes to Hermann High School
- lives in a big city on the Hudson River
- has a mother who is a TV reporter
- is interested in farming
- takes part in TYCTWD
- speaks English and Spanish
- has a mom called Josephine
- speaks English and German
- lives on the Californian coast
- has a girlfriend called Cindy
- had to raise money for the trip to the Grand Canyon
- visited Las Vegas in the summer vacation

b) Write answers (one word). Then write a letter from each answer, as in the example.

1 Timo's family leaves Germany and goes to live here. Hermann (3) R

2 Over 85% of America's ... are produced in California. ________ (10) ____

3 US school grade 'C' means ... ________ (1) ____

4 The AE word for 'biscuit' is ... ________ (3) ____

5 Another word for 'Latino' is ... ________ (5) ____

6 Pacific, Mountain, Central and Eastern are the names of US time ... ________ (1) ____

7 Before the Civil War, black slaves worked on the cotton ... in the South. ________ (4) ____

▶ *Put the letters in the correct order to find the name of a US state that the four students have all visited:*

____

c) Who says it where? On which pages in your student's book can you find these sentences? Write a name and a page number.

	Speaker	Page
1 I'm in FFA because it gives you a lot of experience.	Jake	57
2 I feel very lucky to live in America, where you can succeed if you have the right attitude.		
3 It might be dangerous. I'll drop you off at Dad's on the way.		
4 I know. Let's walk over to the fire station and say hi to Dad.		
5 We sang songs in Spanish and English the whole time – till the driver said we had to stop.		

Now add the page numbers together: ________. If you get 196, your answers are correct.

1 Write the missing words.

1 Madison's mom works for the TV news ____________ CNN.

2 Madison's favourite programmes are weekly crime and drama ____________ .

3 The main time when people watch TV in the evenings is called ____________ time .

4 Madison's dad was ____________ because she knew the date of Martin Luther King's death.

5 Shirley Franklin was elected first black woman ____________ of Atlanta in 2002.

5901 6 Martin Luther King, leader of the US ____________ Movement, came from Atlanta.

2 During or while?

1 The phone rang three times ____________ Madison was watching her favourite programme.

5902 2 The phone rang three times ____________ Madison's favourite programme.

3 Since or for?

Madison has been at her friend's ...

1 ________ 4 o'clock. 2 ________ at least three hours.

5903 3 ________ ages. 4 ________ this morning.

4 Ask questions with How long ...?

1 Madison is at the shopping mall. – How long ____________ there?

2 The Youngs have a new TV. – How long ____________ it?

5904 3 Mr Young works at the MLK Center. – How long ____________ there?

5 STUDY SKILLS Research

Find and tick (✓) the five correct statements.

When you look for information on the internet or in books, ...

- use only one good source ____
- use at least one English source ____
- say what your sources are ____
- 5905 take notes in full sentences ____
- use more than one source ____
- think of the 5 Ws ____
- use your own words ____

20 points

Now you

5906 5907 *How much TV do you watch every day? When do you watch? What kind of programmes do you watch and why? Write about television and you (about 100 words) in your exercise book.*

Jetzt kann ich ...	Sehr gut!	OK	Verbessern!
HÖREN: Ich kann ...			
... längere Texte und Geschichten verstehen, auch wenn ich einige Wörter nicht kenne.	☐	☐	☐
... aus Listenings (z.B. öffentliche Durchsagen) Details richtig heraushören.	☐	☐	☐
... den Akzent britischer und amerikanischer Sprecher/innen heraushören.	☐	☐	☐
SPRECHEN: Ich kann ...			
... anhand von Bildern eine Stadt und ihre Umgebung beschreiben.	☐	☐	☐
... meine Meinung zu Themen im Unterricht (z.B. gesunde Lebensmittel und Essgewohnheiten, Unterschiede zwischen amerikanischen und deutschen Schulen) frei äußern, auch wenn ich Fehler mache.	☐	☐	☐
... über Filme und Fernsehsendungen sprechen.	☐	☐	☐
LESEN: Ich ...			
... weiß, wie man die Hauptaussage (*main idea*), die Beispiele (*examples*) und die Begründungen (*reasons*) in einem Sachtext erkennen kann.	☐	☐	☐
... kann in einem Sachtext Schlussfolgerungen aus gesammelten Fakten ziehen, wobei sich die Fakten an verschiedenen Stellen im Text befinden können.	☐	☐	☐
... kann eine *timeline* geschichtlicher Ereignisse richtig verstehen.	☐	☐	☐
SCHREIBEN: Ich kann ...			
... eine Zusammenfassung (*summary*) einer Geschichte schreiben, indem ich die Hauptereignisse und das Wichtigste zu den 5 Ws mit eigenen Worten wiedergebe. Detaillierte Beschreibungen und direkte Rede lasse ich weg.	☐	☐	☐
... eine Geschichte zu Ende schreiben.	☐	☐	☐
... eine E-mail über einen Film oder eine Fernsehsendung schreiben.	☐	☐	☐
... einen Brief mit der Bitte um Informationen verfassen.	☐	☐	☐
LAND UND LEUTE: Ich ...			
... weiß vieles über das Leben an einer amerikanischen *high school* (z.B. typische Fächer, das Notensystem A–F).	☐	☐	☐
... weiß, was *extracurriculars* sind und dass sie an amerikanischen *high schools* sehr wichtig sind.	☐	☐	☐
... habe einiges über Hermann und Missouri gelernt (z.B. Bevölkerung, Größe, Landschaft, Industrie, Geschichte).	☐	☐	☐
... weiß, dass in Hermann deutsche Traditionen (z.B. Volksfeste) gepflegt werden.	☐	☐	☐
... habe viel über die Stadt Atlanta und ihre Geschichte gelernt.	☐	☐	☐
... habe einiges über Martin Luther King und die Geschichte der *Civil Rights Movement* gelernt.	☐	☐	☐

Jetzt kann ich ...

	Sehr gut!	OK	Verbessern!
GRAMMATIKVERSTÄNDNIS: Ich kann ...			
... einige Nomen, die im Englischen keine Pluralform haben, richtig verwenden (z.B. *furniture/homework/information/news is ...*). Mit solchen nicht zählbaren Nomen verwende ich die Mengenangaben *some/any, a lot of/(not) much.*	☐	☐	☐
... den bestimmten Artikel richtig einsetzen. Wenn ein Nomen für einen abstrakten Begriff (z.B. *life, quality, health*) oder eine Stoffbezeichnung (z.B. *air, oil*) ganz allgemein gebraucht wird, steht es ohne *the*. *The* verwende ich bei solchen Nomen, wenn sie näher bestimmt werden (z.B. *Life is exciting for Timo. / The life of Missouri farmers is interesting.*).	☐	☐	☐
... mit dem *present progressive* über feste Pläne und Verabredungen in der Zukunft sprechen, auch 'Kalender-Zukunft' genannt (z.B. *On Friday after school I'm meeting some friends in town.*).	☐	☐	☐
... das *present perfect* mit *since* und *for* verstehen und richtig anwenden. Damit drücke ich einen Zustand aus, der in der Vergangenheit begonnen hat und jetzt noch andauert. Mit *since* gebe ich einen Zeitpunkt an. Mit *for* gebe ich einen Zeitraum an (z.B. *I've known Kim since 2005/ for five years.*).	☐	☐	☐
VOKABELVERSTÄNDNIS: Ich kann ...			
... AE-Wörter für die Schule (z.B. *elementary school, middle school, schedule, grades, extracurriculars*) richtig verwenden.	☐	☐	☐
... Wörter für Lebensmittel (z.B. *muesli, beans, poultry, whole-grain products*) richtig verwenden.	☐	☐	☐
... Wörter für *media*, insbesondere Fernsehen (z.B. *prime time, crime series, rerun, documentary, channels*) richtig verwenden.	☐	☐	☐
... Adjektive mit der Endung *-able* richtig bilden (z.B. *breakable, doable*).	☐	☐	☐
SKILLS – LERNEN UND ARBEITEN: Ich ...			
... weiß, dass man beim Recherchieren mehrere Quellen benutzt und Notizen mit eigenen Worten schreibt.	☐	☐	☐
... weiß, wie ich das Internet mithilfe von gut gewählten *key words* erfolgreich zur Recherche nutzen kann.	☐	☐	☐

WAS ICH FÜR MEIN ENGLISCHLERNEN GETAN HABE: Ich habe ...	häufig	manchmal	nie
... die Angaben im Grammar File in meinem Buch aufmerksam gelesen.	☐	☐	☐
... versucht, die Lern- und Arbeitstechniken im Skills File in meinem Buch im Unterricht und bei den Hausaufgaben gezielt anzuwenden.	☐	☐	☐
... bereits gelernte Vokabeln und Grammatik häufig aufgefrischt.	☐	☐	☐

WIE ICH MICH VERBESSERN KÖNNTE: Ich könnte ...

- ... im Unterricht aktiver mitarbeiten. ☐
- ... häufiger ein zweisprachiges Wörterbuch verwenden. ☐
- ... gezielt englische Websites zu Unterrichtsthemen recherchieren. ☐
- ... mir Notizen auf Englisch von englischsprachigen Websites machen. ☐
- ... mir häufiger die Texte auf meiner CD anhören. ☐

1 WORDS Lists ▸ *after Unit 1*

Find and write the group words or phrases at the top of the lists. Then write the words in the correct list.

transport • championship • tube • sport • people • ambulance • editor • holidays
sights • paramedic • ferry • abroad • ski slope • tram • suitcase • plane
running track • neighbour • tent • helicopter • goalkeeper • adult • stadium • husband
motel • athletics • presenter • beach

1 Transport	2 S	3 P	4 H
tube			

6201

2 Questions (Simple present) ▸ *after Unit 1*

Make questions with question words. Use the words in brackets and the simple present.

1 Caitlin lives in New York. (Madison?) Where does Madison live?
2 Madison comes from Atlanta. (Jake?) ______
3 Caitlin likes cycling and hiking (Madison and Luis?) ______
4 Luis speaks two languages. (Jake?) ______
6202 5 Jake starts school at 8.20. (Luis and Caitlin?) ______

3 Get it right! Spelling: *-ing*-forms ▸ *after Unit 1*

Write the -ing-forms of the verbs in the correct lists.

run • stop • try • get • swim • lose • walk
joke • take • change • use • wear • win • call • hurry

+ ing	~~e~~ + ing	2x + ing
calling	changing	getting

4 The taxi is waiting (Simple present or present progressive) ▸ *after Unit 1*

Complete with the correct form of the verb in brackets: simple present or present progressive.

Mum Come on! Hurry! The taxi _is waiting_ (wait). We _have to_ (have to) leave for the airport now.

Sam I ____________ (still, pack) my bag. The plane ____________ (not leave) until lunchtime. Why ____________ (Mum, always, get) nervous every time we ____________ (go) on holiday?

Ann Well, something usually ____________ (go) wrong. Somebody ____________ (always, forget) something.

Sam Oh. But Dad ____________ (not get) nervous, does he? What ____________ (he, do) just now?

Ann He ____________ (already, sit) in the taxi, I ____________ (think).

6304 *Dad* Well, no, I ____________ (not sit) in the taxi. Erm ... I ____________ (look) for my passport[1] ...

5 When did you go? (Simple past: questions) ▸ *after Unit 1*

Make questions. Use the words in brackets and the simple past.

1 A: I went to the USA in June. (When?) – B: _When did you go?_

2 A: I stayed in San Francisco. (Where?) – B: ____________

3 A: I stayed there for three weeks. (How long?) – B: ____________

6305 4 A: I saw lots of famous sights. (What?) – B: ____________

6 We went up the Stratosphere Tower (Simple past) ▸ *after Unit 1*

Complete the dialogue with simple past forms of the verbs in brackets.

Kate Tom! You're back! How _was_ (be) your trip to Las Vegas? _Did you have_ (you, have) a good time?

Tom Oh, yes, thanks. I ____________ (have) a great time.

Kate So where ____________ (you, go) and what ____________ (you, see)?

Tom Well, I ____________ (do) a tour of all the theme hotels with my cousin Eli, and my aunt and uncle ____________ (plan) a day tour to Death Valley for me. It was awesome.

Kate And what ____________ (you, do) in the evenings?

Tom One evening we ____________ (go) up the Stratosphere Tower. I ____________ (not enjoy) going up in the fast lift much. I just ____________ (close) my eyes and ____________ (try) to think of something else. But I ____________ (take) some cool photos from the top.

6306

[1] passport ['pɑːspɔːt] *Reisepass*

7 It was raining (Simple past or past progressive) ► after Unit 1

Underline the correct verb form.

1 When we (were arriving/arrived) in New York, it (rained/was raining).

2 The sun suddenly (came/was coming) out when we (were taking/took) photos of the Statue of Liberty.

3 We (saw/were seeing) lots of interesting people when we (were walking/walked) through Central Park.

4 Just as I (was crossing/crossed) Times Square, a man (was asking/asked) me something in German.

5 Yesterday we (cycled/were cycling) onto Brooklyn Bridge and (watched/were watching) the boats below.

6407 6 As I (was shopping/shopped) in Macy's, I suddenly (realized[1]/was realizing) that I had forgotten my money.

8 WORDS People or things? ► after Unit 1

Write the words in two groups.

adult • cooker • counter • elevator • firefighter • guy • hijacker • hostess • immigrant • laughter • leader • leather • mirror • murder • murderer • painter • pepper • quarter • skyscraper • sleepover • supporter • ticket agent • waiter • writer

People: adult, __________

Things: cooker, __________

9 Get it right! Verbs: irregular verb forms ► after Unit 1 • pp. 250–251

Complete the lists with verb forms.

• become	• became	• become	• ____	• ____	• forgotten
• ____	• ____	• chosen	• hold	• ____	• ____
• come	• ____	• ____	• ring	• ____	• ____
• ____	• drank	• ____	• ____	• ____	• stood
• fall	• ____	• ____	• ____	• ____	• taught
• ____	• ____	• felt	• ____	• wore	• ____
• fly	• ____	• ____	• ____	• ____	• written

[1] realize ['riːəlaɪz] *bemerken*

10 They've all been there (Simple past or present perfect) ► *after Unit 1*

Complete with the simple past or the present perfect.

Lucy, Brad and Kelly *have all been* (all, be) to the Grand Canyon. They *went* (go) there in the last summer vacation. Here's what they ____________ (say) after their trip.

Kelly The Grand Canyon is the most exciting place I ____________ (ever, see).
And walking on the glass floor is the scariest thing I ____________ (ever, do) in my life.

Lucy We ____________ (stay) at the Canyon for three days. I ____________ (never, see) anything so beautiful. It ____________ (be) so awesome!

Brad If you ____________ (not be) to the Grand Canyon, you really must go.
We ____________ (enjoy) every minute of the trip. I ____________ (visit) some cool places in the US, but nothing like the Grand Canyon.

6510

11 If I have enough money, ... (Conditional sentences 1 and 2) ► *after Unit 1*

Complete the sentences with the correct form of the verb.

1 A: If I *have* (have) enough money in summer, maybe I *'ll go* (go) to the USA with a friend.

2 B: Great! Where ____________ (you, stay) if you go?

3 A: Well, maybe California, for three weeks. We'd take our camping gear if we ____________ (stay) at places along the coast.

4 B: Cool. You ____________ (be able to) swim in the Pacific every day if you were close to a beach.
If I ever ____________ (visit) California, I'd want to see the theme parks[1], Disneyland or SeaWorld.

6512

5 A: That would be cool too. But if we went to theme parks, we ____________ all our money in the first week!

[1] theme park ['θiːm pɑːk] *Themenpark (Freizeitpark)*

12 Greg's presentation (have to, be allowed to, be able to) ▸ *after Unit 1*

Complete with the correct form of the modal in brackets: simple present, simple past or will-future.

I *have to* (have to) give a presentation about George Washington, but my computer is broken. Dad is in London and I ______ (not be allowed to) use his computer when he isn't at home. Yesterday I ______ (have to) go to the library. I ______ (be able to) get some information, but not enough. I ______ (have to) ask my friend for help tomorrow. I hope he ______ (be able to) download some stuff for me. If I don't finish my presentation, I ______ (not be allowed) go to the disco next Saturday.

13 WORDS Word families (Nouns from verbs) ▸ *after Unit 1*

Write a noun from each verb. Sometimes the noun is the same as the verb. If you know two nouns, write both.

	Verb		Noun		Verb		Noun
1	announce	–	*announcement*	9	explain	–	______
2	argue	–	______	10	fly	–	______
3	arrive	–	______	11	hope	–	______
4	begin	–	______	12	invite	–	______
5	collect	–	______	13	joke	–	______
6	cook	–	______	14	live	–	______
7	depart	–	______	15	mix	–	______
8	discuss	–	______	16	murder	–	______

14 Ride carefully! (Adjective or adverb) ▸ *after Unit 1*

Complete with the adjective or adverb form of the word in brackets.

1 My dad is a taxi-driver in New York, so he knows the city traffic *well* (good).

2 He always tells me to ride ______ (careful) when I'm on my bike.

3 He says most people drive ______ (safe), but there are always some ______ (bad) drivers who go too ______ (fast).

4 You have to be ______ (careful) on the sidewalks too. Some kids skate ______ (dangerous), so you're not ______ (safe) anywhere in a big city, says my dad. He worries too much.

6203

15 USA: People and places (who or that) ▸ *after Unit 1*

*Complete the sentences with **who** or **that**.*

1 New York and San Francisco are the cities *that* European tourists want to visit most.

2 Michael Phelps is the swimmer ________ won 8 gold medals for the USA in the 2008 Olympic Games.

3 Beach volleyball is a sport ________ first came from California. It's now an Olympic team sport.

4 Frédéric-Auguste Bartholdi was born in France in 1834. He is the man ________ designed the Statue of Liberty.

5 Florida is the only state ________ has two rivers with the same name: the Withlacoochee. There's one in the north and one in central Florida.

6716 6 Theodore (Teddy) Roosevelt was the US president ________ gave the teddy bear its name in 1902.

16 The Grand Canyon (Contact clauses) ▸ *after Unit 1*

*a) Find six sentences where you don't need **who** or **that**. Write them again as contact clauses. You need the letters in brackets in b).*

US Park Rangers protect the animals that live in the National Parks (J) and the tourists who visit every year (N). There is lots of information that the Rangers can give you (A). For example, they can tell you about the Native Americans who first lived in the Canyon area (N). In National Parks there are lots of things that tourists must or mustn't do (E). There are rules that you must follow if you want to be safe (A). One rule says you mustn't make fires in places that can be dangerous (D).
There are lots of things that you can do at Grand Canyon National Park. (D). There's a free shuttle bus that you can take along the rim (N). There are mule trains that take you down to the Canyon floor (H). If you want to hike, there are trails that are easy and safe (A). There are also trails that tourists mustn't take if they aren't fit (V).

1 *There is lots of information the Rangers can give you.* ________ *A*

2 ________ ________

3 ________ ________

4 ________ ________

5 ________ ________

6 ________ ________

b) Write down the letters in brackets after your six sentences. Then put them in the right order to find the name of a US state.

6717 The state is ▶ ________.

17 Find the mistakes

▸ after Unit 1 • SF (p. 147)

Find and correct the mistakes in Heike's postcard to her cousin in the US.

Hello Rachel,

We stay here in Hamburg for one week. Just now we sit in a café, so I write postcards. Yesterday we have taken a boat trip round the harbour and in the evening we have seen a musical. It's nice here. If you would come to visit Germany, you'd like it here too, I think. Maybe tomorrow we go to the famous Hamburg Michel. It's a church with a big clock tower, who all the tourists climb. Mum want to go to a museum – but I don't enjoy to look round museums!

Love, Heike

are staying, ____________

____

____

____

____

____

____

____

18 WORDS Odd one out

▸ after Unit 1

a) *Find and write the odd one out. Then count and write the letters.*

1	trousers	shorts	jeans	clothes	clothes	(3)	o
2	pepper	flower	supporter	elevator		(5)	
3	cow	turkey	bacon	pig		(2)	
4	California	Missouri	Ontario	Georgia		(4)	
5	ranger	cooker	photographer	caretaker		(4)	
6	went	saw	swum	wrote		(4)	
7	drum	flute	trumpet	ceilidh		(7)	
8	cathedral	synagogue	mosque	hostel		(6)	

b) *Put the letters in the right order and find the word that completes the sentence:*

▶ On their way to the Grand Canyon, Jake and his dad drove through ______ ____________.

19 I had never been to the USA (Simple past or past perfect) ▸ *after Unit 1*

Underline the correct verb form.

1 Last year we (went/had gone) to New York. I was excited because I (had never been/never went) to the USA before.

2 When we (arrived/had arrived) at JFK, I wasn't tired because I (slept/had slept) on the plane.

3 But after we (had waited/waited) an hour for our bags, I (was/had been) tired.

4 We (went/had gone) for something to eat after we (found/had found) our hotel.

5 I (didn't eat/hadn't eaten) much because I (already ate/had already eaten) my lunch and most of mum's lunch on the plane.

6920 6 It (was/had been) good that we didn't eat much. Dad couldn't pay the waiter because he (left/had left) his money in the hotel.

20 WORDS Word fields ▸ *after Unit 1*

How many words can you add to the word fields? Look at the pictures for help and use the Dictionary in your student's book (pp. 189–219).

In a National Park	Downtown

1 In a National Park: *river, hiking trail,* ______________________

____

____

____

2 Downtown: *shopping mall,* ______________________

____

____

____

____

- Hier kannst du deine Antworten im Checkpoint überprüfen. Falls du Probleme mit den jeweiligen Aufgaben hattest, folge den Lernhilfen in der rechten Spalte. Die Verweise beziehen sich auf dein Schülerbuch oder dein Workbook.
- Deine Punktzahl kannst du ermitteln, indem du dir für jede richtige Lösung einen Punkt gibst. Schreib deine Gesamtpunktzahl in das gelbe Kästchen unten links.

1 Write the names of the places.

6 P.

1 deli
2 downtown
3 skyscraper(s)
4 block
5 apartment
6 gas station

- Lies dir im Skills File in deinem Buch den Abschnitt zu *Learning words* durch (S. 138).
- Lern die Wörter mithilfe des Vocabulary (Buch: S. 169–174).

2 Find and write six pairs.

6 P.

1 ground floor – first floor
2 holiday(s) – vacation
3 pavement – sidewalk
4 queue – line
5 timetable – schedule
6 year – grade

- Lern die unterschiedlichen BE- und AE-Wörter mithilfe der blauen Kästen auf den S. 170 und 172 in deinem Buch.

3 If or when?

3 P.

1 when 2 if 3 when

- Wiederhole die Übung 11 im Practice-Teil (Buch: S. 24).

4 Complete the sentences with gerunds.

5 P.

1 planning
2 meeting
3 finding
4 taking
5 travelling

- Schau dir Grammar File 1 zum Gerundium in deinem Buch (S. 155–156) oder hinten im Skills File *kompakt* in deinem Workbook (S. 76–77) noch einmal an.
- Löse die Aufgaben 4a/c, 5a (S. 21) und 6a (S. 22) im Practice-Teil in deinem Buch.

Now you (Ideas)

Good things: a rich, multi-cultural city with world-famous sights/important tourist centre/ interesting history (Ellis Island, Liberty etc)/ a lot to see: Broadway theatres, concerts, opera, famous museums, art galleries/Central Park/ international airports/subway/a city that never sleeps is exciting

Bad things: traffic day and night/noise/busy city streets often dirty/can take a long time to get around/ poor areas (e.g. the Bronx)/ expensive city to live in/ high prices for houses and apartments

- Um Ideen über New York zu sammeln, kannst du dir die Unit 1 in deinem Buch noch einmal anschauen oder im Internet recherchieren.
- Lies dir im Skills File den Abschnitt zu *Brainstorming* durch (Buch: S. 144), um deine Ideen besser ordnen zu können.
- Um den Gebrauch des *simple present* sicherer zu beherrschen, kannst du im Revision-Block in deinem Workbook die Übungen 2 (S. 62) und 4 (S. 63) machen.
- Trage deinen kurzen Vortrag über New York laut vor.

Ich habe ____ Punkte von 20.

20–18	Sehr gut. Weiter so!
17–15	Schon recht gut.
Unter 15	Genauer lernen!

1 Write the missing words.

1 bilingual
2 minority
3 illegal
4 attitude
5 prejudiced
6 opinion

6 P.

2 Complete the word families.

1 experience
2 production
3 industrial
4 succeed
5 discrimination
6 plant

6 P.

3 Complete the sentences with the passive.

1 are grown
2 was first found
3 is produced
4 were killed

4 P.

4 Complete with skim or scan.

1 skim
2 scan
3 scan
4 skim

4 P.

Now you (Ideas)

For many people California is a dreamland because ... sunny weather all year/beautiful National Parks/rich multi-cultural state

Industries: farming (fruit and vegetables), Silicon Valley (computer and software industry), movie industry/ theme parks

Tourist activities: enjoy beautiful beaches/drive along the coast/go surfing/visit National Parks/visit theme parks/see cities like San Francisco and L.A. with many tourist attractions

Problems of the state: danger of earthquakes/forest fires almost every year/homeless people/illegal immigrants

Ich habe ______ Punkte von 20.

20–18	Sehr gut. Weiter so!
17–15	Schon recht gut.
Unter 15	Genauer lernen!

Falls du Probleme hattest:

- Guck dir im Skills File in deinem Buch den Abschnitt zu *Learning words* an (S. 138).
- Lern die Wörter (Buch: S. 174–178).

- Schau dir die Wörter noch einmal im Vocabulary an und lern sie (Buch: S. 174–178).
- Im Revision-Block gibt es auch eine Übung zu *word families* (Workbook: S. 66, Übung 13).

- Lies dir Grammar File 2a–c zum Passiv noch einmal durch (Buch: S. 157, Workbook: S. 77).
- Löse die Aufgaben 8–10 im Practice-Teil (Buch: S. 45).

- Im Skills File kannst du dir die wichtigen Punkte zu *skimming* und *scanning* noch einmal anschauen (Buch: S. 150, Workbook: S. 75).
- Mach die Übung 4 im Practice-Teil noch einmal (Buch: S. 43).

- Suche in der Unit 2 in deinem Buch nach Informationen über die relevanten Punkte über Kalifornien. Du kannst auch im Internet recherchieren.
- Die *writing skills* kannst du dir im Skills File noch einmal anschauen (Buch: S. 146–147, Workbook: S. 74).
- Um sicherer bei Beschreibungen zu werden, kannst du im Revision-Block die Übungen 14–16 machen (Workbook: S. 66–67).

1 Write the missing words.

6 P.

1 sister city
2 wine
3 Government
4 apply for
5 average
6 cheerleaders

2 Put in a/an, some, much or many.

5 P.

1 much some an
2 many some

3 Add the where you need it.

4 P.

1 Jake: the
Timo: –
2 – The

4 Find and tick (✓) the five correct statements.

5 P.

- give only the most important information from the original text. ✓
- tell the reader what the text or story is about in the first few sentences. ✓
- explain **who** does **what**, **where**, **when** and **why**. ✓
- leave out examples and direct speech. ✓
- give lots of details. ___
- use the simple present and your own words. ✓
- use lots of adjectives for description and comparisons. ___

Now you (Ideas)

There are a few important differences between US and German schools. First, ... US school types: elementary, junior high, high school/school day is longer (afternoon school until 3 pm every day)/ hot lunch in school/US grade system (A–F)/ different classrooms for different subjects – students go to the classrooms/school bus for students/ longer summer vacation, about 3 months/extracurricular activities and sports are important/ cheerleaders for school teams

Ich habe ______ Punkte von 20.

20–18 Sehr gut. Weiter so!
17–15 Schon recht gut.
Unter 15 Genauer lernen!

Falls du Probleme hattest:

- Lies dir im Skills File den Abschnitt zu *Learning words* durch (Buch: S. 138).
- Lern die Wörter mithilfe des Vocabulary (Buch: S. 179–184).

- Über die Besonderheiten von nicht zählbaren Nomen erfährst du etwas im Grammar File 3 (Buch: S. 159, Workbook: S. 78).
- Wiederhole die Übungen 6 und 7 im Practice-Teil (Buch: S. 64).

- Wie du den bestimmten Artikel *the* gebrauchst, erfährst du im Grammar File 4 (Buch: S. 160, Workbook: S. 79).
- Löse die Aufgabe 10 im Practice-Teil (Buch: S. 66).

- Im Skills File kannst du noch einmal nachlesen, was beim *summary writing* wichtig ist (Buch: S. 145).
- Schau dir auch den blauen Kasten auf S. 67 in deinem Buch an.

- Informationen über amerikanische Schulen findest du in der Unit 3 in deinem Buch und in den Aufgaben 3–5 in deinem Workbook (S. 35–36).
- Ordne deine Gedanken und strukturiere deinen Text in sinnvolle Absätze (*Writing course*: Buch S. 146–147, Workbook S. 74).

Falls du Probleme hattest:

1 Write the missing words.

1 *network*
2 *series*
3 *prime*
4 *impressed*
5 *mayor*
6 *Civil Rights*

6 P.

- Lern die Wörter (Buch: S. 184–188).

2 During or while?

1 *while*
2 *during*

2 P.

- Im blauen Kasten auf S. 184 in deinem Buch kannst du nachlesen, wann du *during* und wann du *while* benutzen musst.

3 Since or for?

1 *since*
2 *for*
3 *for*
4 *since*

4 P.

- Lies dir Grammar File 6 noch einmal durch (Buch: S. 162, Workbook: S. 80).
- Schau dir auch den blauen Kasten zu 'seit' auf S. 186 in deinem Buch an.
- Löse die Aufgaben 9 und 10a/b im Practice-Teil (Buch: S. 88–89).

4 Ask questions with How long ...?

1 How long *has she been* there?
2 How long *have they had* it?
3 How long *has he worked* there?

3 P.

- Schau dir Grammar File 6 an (Buch: S. 162, Workbook: S. 80).
- Mach auch die Aufgaben 9 und 10 im Revision-Block, damit du das *present perfect* sicherer beherrscht (Workbook: S. 64–65).

5 STUDY SKILLS Research

- use only one good source
- use more than one source ✓
- use at least one English source ✓
- think of the 5 Ws ✓
- take notes in full sentences
- say what your sources are ✓
- use your own words ✓

5 P.

- Im Skills File erfährst du, wie du beim Recherchieren am besten vorgehen solltest (Buch: S. 141).
- Lies dir auch den blauen Kasten zu *research* auf S. 81 in deinem Buch durch.

Now you (Ideas)

I'm (not) a TV fan/ I watch (don't watch) TV every day/ In my free time I like to do other things like sports or going out with friends/I could (couldn't) live without TV/ I watch TV for one to two hours a day/at the weekend/before I go to bed/ after I have done my homework/ I only watch my favourite programmes/I like to watch the news/sports programmes/ a soap opera/documentaries/quiz shows, etc. / I think ... game shows/comedy shows/soap operas, etc. are good/bad/stupid/ interesting/funny

- Wichtige Wörter und Ideen zum Thema *TV* findest du in der Unit 4 in deinem Buch (S. 78).
- Strukturiere deinen Text (*Writing course*: Buch S. 146–147, Workbook S. 74).

Ich habe ______ Punkte von 20.

20–18	Sehr gut. Weiter so!
17–15	Schon recht gut.
Unter 15	Genauer lernen!

MEDIATION SKILLS ▶ *SF p. 143*

Manchmal musst du zwischen zwei Sprachen vermitteln; das nennt man mediation.

- Übersetze nicht alles wörtlich.
- Gib nur das Wesentliche weiter, lass Unwichtiges weg.
- Verwende kurze und einfache Sätze.
- Wenn du ein Wort nicht kennst, umschreibe es oder ersetze es durch ein anderes Wort.

REVISION Writing course – Zusammenfassung ▶ *SF pp. 146–147*

The steps of writing

1. Brainstorming – Ideen sammeln.
2. Schreiben. Dabei achte darauf,
   - deine Sätze zu verbinden und auszubauen *(Writing better sentences)*
   - deinen Text gut zu strukturieren *(Using paragraphs)*
   - bei einem Bericht die 5 Ws abzudecken *(Writing a report)*
3. Deinen Text inhaltlich und sprachlich überprüfen *(Correcting your text)*

Writing better sentences

Eine Geschichte klingt interessanter, wenn man die Sätze mit **linking words** miteinander verbindet. Dabei gibt es mehrere Möglichkeiten:

- **Time phrases** wie at 7 o'clock, every morning, in the afternoons, a few minutes later, suddenly, then, next ...
- **Konjunktionen** wie although, because, but, so ... that, that, when, while ...
- **Relativpronomen** wie that und who
- Mit Adjektiven kannst du eine Person, einen Ort, einen Gegenstand oder ein Erlebnis genauer und interessanter beschreiben. Vergleiche: The man looked into the room. ▶ The young man looked into the empty room.
- Mit Adverbien kannst du beschreiben, **wie** jemand etwas macht: The young man looked nervously into the empty room.

Using paragraphs

Ein längerer Text ist besser zu verstehen, wenn er mehrere Absätze enthält:

- eine Einleitung **(beginning)** – hier schreibst du, worum es geht
- einen Hauptteil **(middle)** – hier schreibst du mehr über dein Thema
- einen Schluss **(end)** – hier bringst du den Text zu einem interessanten Ende.

Am Anfang eines Absatzes sind kurze, einleitende Sätze **(topic sentences)** gut, weil sie den Lesern sofort sagen, worum es geht, z. B.

1. Orte: My trip to ... was fantastic. / ... is famous for ... / ... is a great place.
2. Personen: ... is funny/interesting/clever ...
3. Aktivitäten: ... is good fun. / Lots of people ... every day.

- Beginne mit einem interessanten Einstiegssatz: You'll never guess what happened to me today! / Did I tell you that ...?
- Fang für jeden neuen Aspekt einen neuen Absatz an.
- Beende deinen Text mit einer Zusammenfassung oder etwas Persönlichem.

Writing a report – structuring information

- Gib dem Leser **eine schnelle Orientierung**, was passiert ist.
- Beginne mit **wichtigen Informationen** und gib erst dann Detailinformationen.
- Ein Bericht gibt immer Antworten auf die **5 Ws**: Who? What? When? Where? Why? und manchmal auch auf How?
- Verwende das *simple past*.

Correcting your text

Spelling mistakes

Lies deinen Text langsam, Wort für Wort, Buchstabe für Buchstabe. Wenn du unsicher bist, hilft dir ein Wörterbuch. Beachte folgende Regeln:

Tipp

- Manche Wörter haben Buchstaben, die man nicht spricht, aber schreibt, z. B. autumn, climb.
- Manchmal ändert sich die Schreibweise, wenn ein Wort eine Endung erhält, z. B. take → taking, terrible → terribly, lucky → luckily, try → tries (**aber** stay → stays), run → running, drop → dropped.
- Beim Plural tritt manchmal noch ein -e zum -s, z. B. church → churches.

Grammar mistakes

Diese Tipps helfen dir, typische Fehler zu vermeiden:

Tipp

- Im **simple present** wird in der 3. Person Singular -s angehängt: she knows
- **Unregelmäßige Verben:** Manche Verben bilden die Formen des *simple past* und des Partizip Perfekt *(past participle)* unregelmäßig. Die unregelmäßigen Formen musst du lernen. Die Liste steht auf S. 250–251 in deinem Buch. go – went – gone; buy – bought – bought
- **Verneinung:** Im *simple present* werden Vollverben mit don't/doesn't verneint, im *simple past* mit didn't.
- **Satzstellung**: Im Englischen gilt immer (auch im Nebensatz):
  a) subject – verb – object (SVO) ... when I saw my brother.
  als ich meinen Bruder sah.
  b) Orts- vor Zeitangabe I bought a nice book in the city yesterday.

LISTENING SKILLS

▶ *SF p. 148*

Vor dem Hören:
- Lies dir die Fragen durch. So weißt du, worauf du beim Hören achten musst.
- Nutze Überschriften oder Bilder um zu erahnen, um was es geht.
- Bereite dich darauf vor, Notizen zu machen. Leg z.B. eine Tabelle oder Liste an.

Beim Hören:
- Achte auf Geräusche, unterschiedliche Stimmen und wie Leute sprechen.
- Mach nur kurze Notizen, z.B. Symbole oder Stichworte, keine ganzen Sätze.
- Lass dich nicht verunsichern, wenn du mal einen Satz nicht verstehst.

Nach dem Hören:
- Vervollständige deine Notizen sofort.
- Achte beim zweiten Hören auf das, was du zuerst nicht gut verstanden hast.

Mach dir bewusst, welche Einzelheiten du heraushören sollst bzw. willst. Lass dich von anderen Einzelheiten nicht ablenken.

Manche Signalwörter machen es dir leichter, den Hörtext zu verstehen:
Aufzählung: **and**, **another**, **too**; Gegensatz: **although**, **but**
Grund, Folge: **because**, **so**, **so that**; Vergleich: **larger/older/... than**, **more**, **most**; Reihenfolge: **before**, **after**, **then**, **next**, **later**, **when**, **at last**, **at the same time**

READING COURSE – Zusammenfassung

▶ *SF pp. 150–151*

REVISION Working out the meaning of words

Was hilft mir, unbekannte Wörter zu verstehen?

1. Bilder zeigen oft die Dinge, die du im Text nicht verstehst. Schau sie dir deshalb vor dem Lesen genau an.
2. Oft hilft dir der Textzusammenhang, z.B.
   *When we **reached** the station, Judy went to the ticket machine to buy our tickets.*
3. Zu manchen englischen Wörtern fallen dir vielleicht deutsche, französische oder lateinische Wörter ein, die ähnlich geschrieben oder ausgesprochen werden, z.B. **excellent**, **millionaire**, **nation**, **reality**.
4. Manchmal stecken in unbekannten Wörtern bekannte Teile, z.B. **friendliness**, **helpless**, **understandable**, **gardener**, **tea bag**, **waiting room**.

REVISION Skimming and Scanning

Skimming: Lesen, um sich einen Überblick zu verschaffen

Beim **Skimming** überfliegst du einen Text schnell, um dir einen ersten Eindruck zu verschaffen, worum es geht. Das hilft dir herauszufinden, ob ein Text, den du im Internet oder einem Buch gefunden hast, überhaupt die Informationen enthält, nach denen du (z.B. für ein Referat) suchst. Achte dabei auf
- die **Überschrift**
- die **Zwischenüberschriften** und **hervorgehobene** Wörter oder Sätze
- die **Bilder** und **Bildunterschriften**
- den **ersten** und den **letzten Satz** jedes Absatzes
- **Grafiken**, **Statistiken** und die **Quelle** des Textes

Beim **Scanning** suchst du einen Text nach Schlüsselwörtern *(key words)* ab und liest nur dort genauer, wo du sie findest. Das hilft dir, wenn dich nur bestimmte Aspekte eines Themas interessieren.

Finding the main ideas of a text

Wie finde ich die Hauptaussagen eines Textes?

1. Jeder Text dreht sich um ein Thema oder hat eine Hauptaussage, z.B. *Drinking soda is one of the worst things you can do to your health.*
   Diese Hauptaussage findest du oft im **ersten Absatz**. Lies ihn deshalb besonders gründlich durch.
2. Die Hauptaussage wird in der Regel durch weitere Aussagen bzw. Gedanken unterstützt, z.B.
   Experts agree that sugary soft drinks and fast food are the main reasons why so many American teenagers are fat. Du findest sie oft im ersten oder letzten Satz der nachfolgenden Absätze.
3. Diese weiteren Aussagen bzw. Gedanken werden oft durch Beispiele und Begründungen ergänzt, z.B.
   About 7% of the calories that they take in come from soft drinks alone.

Tipp

Die folgenden Wörter oder Ausdrücke werden oft im Zusammenhang mit Begründungen oder Beispielen verwendet:
... % of ... are ... • and so • because • e.g. • etc. • for example • for lots of reasons • this shows that • that's why

Drawing conclusions

Wie funktioniert schlussfolgerndes Lesen?

1. Die einfachste Form des schlussfolgernden Lesens besteht darin, die Informationen aus verschiedenen Textstellen zusammenzuführen. Im Text auf S. 87 in deinem Buch z.B. musst du mehrere Textstellen anschauen, wenn du alle Gründe finden willst, warum Schüler/innen in den USA arbeiten gehen.
2. Manchmal steht die Antwort auf eine Frage nicht direkt im Text. Dann musst du sie dir erschließen. Im Text auf S. 87 geht es um die Frage, welche Auswirkungen das Arbeiten auf die schulischen Leistungen hat. Dafür musst du Fakten im Text finden, die etwas mit dieser Frage zu tun haben:

FACTS: students have an 11 hour work day; after work they're often too tired to do their homework = negative effects
working makes students more disciplined; they learn to organize their time = positive effects
CONCLUSION: for some students it's good, but for many it means bad grades

Unit 1

GF 1 The gerund ► *GF pp. 155–156*

a) Use and form

Flying is exciting.
Fliegen ist aufregend.
Travelling makes me tired.
Reisen macht mich müde.

Taking **a taxi** is quite expensive.
Mit dem Taxi zu fahren / Taxifahren ist ziemlich teuer.
Cycling **in New York** can be dangerous.
In New York Rad zu fahren / Radfahren in New York kann gefährlich sein.

Wenn die *-ing*-Form eines Verbs im Satz die Funktion eines **Nomens** hat, wird sie **Gerundium** *(gerund)* genannt.
Die *-ing*-Form wird, wie du weißt, durch Anhängen von *-ing* an den Infinitiv gebildet: ***fly*** → ***flying***.

Wie ein Verb kann das Gerundium erweitert werden, z.B. durch ein Objekt *(a taxi)* oder eine Orts- oder Zeitangabe *(in New York)*.
Im Deutschen wird das Gerundium oft durch einen Infinitiv mit „zu" oder durch ein Nomen wiedergegeben.

b) The gerund as subject and object

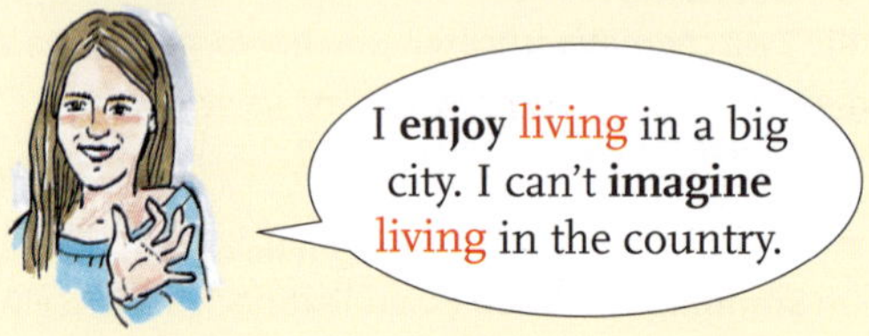

Ich wohne gern in einer Großstadt. / Ich genieße es, in einer Großstadt zu wohnen. Ich kann mir nicht vorstellen, auf dem Land zu leben.

When I got to Times Square, it **started** raining. / to rain.

I **like/love** riding / to ride my bike in the rain.

I'**d like/love** to ride in a New York taxi too.
I **would hate** to live in the country.

Das Gerundium (und seine Erweiterung) kann wie ein Nomen **Subjekt** oder **Objekt** eines Satzes sein:

Subjekt	
Flying	*is exciting.*
Cycling in a big city	*isn't very healthy.*

	Objekt
My sister likes	***skating.***
I like	***riding my bike in Central Park.***

! Beachte:

◄ **1** Nach einigen Verben – z.B. ***enjoy, finish, imagine, miss, practise*** – muss ein weiteres Verb als Gerundium stehen:
*I **enjoy** living ..., I can't **imagine** living ...*

Anders als im Deutschen darf nach diesen Verben **kein Infinitiv** stehen!
Also nicht: *I ~~enjoy to live~~ ..., I can't ~~imagine to live~~ ...*

◄ **2** Nach ***begin/start, continue, hate, like, love*** kann – bei gleicher Bedeutung – ein Gerundium oder ein *to*-Infinitiv stehen.

◄ **3** Nach ***would** like, **would** love, **would** hate* kann nur der *to*-Infinitiv stehen.

c) The gerund after prepositions

After so much walking, we were tired.
Nach all der Herumlauferei ... /
Nachdem wir so viel herumgelaufen waren, ...

Never cross a street without looking.
Überquere nie eine Straße, ohne zu schauen.

Ryan is **scared** of going in lifts.
Ryan hat Angst davor, mit dem Lift zu fahren.

Ryan had often **dreamed** of seeing New York from above. ... davon geträumt, New York von oben zu sehen.

Nach einer Präposition *(after, without, for, of, ...)* muss ein Verb als Gerundium stehen.

Beachte die unterschiedlichen Entsprechungen im Deutschen:

englisch	deutsch
– ***after walking***	→ **Präposition + Nomen** („nach ...") *oder* **Nebensatz** („nachdem ...")
– ***without looking***	→ „ohne zu" + **Infinitiv**
– *scared **of going***	→ „zu" + **Infinitiv**

Ryan is **interested** in learning about New York firefighters.
Ryan ist daran interessiert, etwas über ... zu erfahren.

He's **excited** about meeting some of them.
Er freut sich sehr darauf, einige von ihnen zu treffen.

Nützliche Wendungen mit Präposition + Gerundium sind:

– *(to) be* ***interested in / excited about / afraid of / good/bad at / tired of*** ***doing** sth.*

Ryan had the **chance** of going to New York.
Ryan hatte die Möglichkeit, nach New York zu fahren.

His **reason** for going there was to visit family.
Sein Grund, dort hinzufahren, war ...

Caitlin **was** against going to Brooklyn Bridge.
Caitlin war dagegen, zur Brooklyn Bridge zu gehen.

Ryan and Caitlin **talked** about meeting Ruth.
Ryan und Caitlin sprachen darüber, Ruth zu treffen.

–	*the*	***chance of*** ***reason for*** ***idea of*** ***danger of***	***doing** sth.*
–	*(to)*	***be against*** ***talk about*** ***think of*** ***worry about***	***doing** sth.*

Unit 2

GF 2 The passive

▸ *GF pp. 157–158*

a) Active and passive

Active: **Farmers in California** grow strawberries on large farms.
Landwirte in Kalifornien bauen Erdbeeren auf großen Farmen an.

Passive: **Strawberries** are grown on large farms.
Erdbeeren werden auf großen Farmen angebaut.

Mit einem **Aktivsatz** drückst du aus, **wer oder was etwas tut**. Das Subjekt des Aktivsatzes führt die Handlung aus:

Subjekt	**Verb** (aktiv)	**Objekt**
Farmers in California	*grow*	*strawberries ...*

Mit einem **Passivsatz** drückst du aus, **mit wem oder womit etwas geschieht**. Das Objekt des Aktivsatzes *(strawberries)* ist Subjekt des Passivsatzes geworden:

Subjekt	**Verb** (passiv)	
Strawberries	*are grown*	*on large farms.*

b) Form

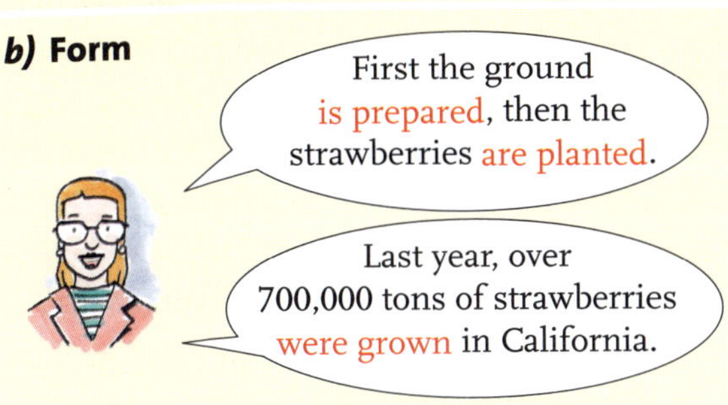

... wird aufbereitet .../... werden gepflanzt .../... wurden angebaut ...

Das Passiv bildest du mit einer **Form von *be*** und der 3. Form des Verbs. Die 3. Form des Verbs heißt **Partizip Perfekt** *(past participle)*.

Simple present:	*am/are/is* + ***past participle***
	*The ground is **prepared** ...*
	*The strawberries are **planted** ...*
Simple past:	*was/were* + ***past participle***
	*700,000 tons were **grown** ...*

c) Use

> At 8.45 yesterday morning a 12-year-old boy was hurt in a car accident on Duke Street. The police were called and the boy was taken to hospital.

Mit einem Passivsatz kannst du Handlungen beschreiben, ohne zu sagen, wer die Handlung ausführt. Oft ist gar nicht bekannt oder nicht wichtig, wer die Handlung ausführt.
Du findest daher das Passiv oft in Nachrichten und in Zeitungsberichten (z. B. über Unfälle, Verbrechen) oder auf Schildern.

Ein englischer Passivsatz wird im Deutschen oft durch einen Aktivsatz mit „man" wiedergegeben:

*The boy **was taken** to hospital.*
***Man brachte** den Jungen ins Krankenhaus.*

d) Passive sentences with *by* ...

The Golden Gate Bridge **was built** by Joseph Strauss.
... wurde von Joseph Strauss erbaut.

The gardener **was attacked** by a dog.
... wurde von einem Hund angefallen.

Wenn du in einem Passivsatz den „Täter" oder „Verursacher" nennen willst, verwendest du die Präposition ***by*** („von", „durch").

e) Extra The passive: *will*-future and modal auxiliaries

Our new attractions will be opened soon.
... werden bald eröffnet (werden).

Sea World can be visited at any time of the year.
... kann das ganze Jahr über besucht werden.

The fire couldn't be put out.
... konnte nicht gelöscht werden.

Passivsätze mit Hilfsverben (z.B. *will, can, could, must, should, must, may*) bildest du mit *be* + Partizip Perfekt:

will	*be*	*opened*
can	*be*	*visited*
could	*be*	*put out*
must	*be*	...
should	*be*	...
may	*be*	...

Unit 3

GF 3 Countable and uncountable nouns

▸ *GF p. 159*

a) Countable nouns

a friend – two friends
a CD – lots of CDs
one hour – many hours

◂ Die meisten Nomen sind **zählbar** – sie bezeichnen etwas, das man zählen kann. Zählbare Nomen kommen im Singular und im Plural vor.

b) Uncountable nouns

bread	Brot	**money**	Geld
butter	Butter	**music**	Musik
furniture	Möbel	**news**	Nachricht(en)
homework	Hausaufgabe(n)	**sugar**	Zucker
information	Information(en)	**traffic**	Verkehr
jewellery	Schmuck	**water**	Wasser
milk	Milch	**work**	Arbeit

◂ **Nicht zählbare** Nomen dagegen bezeichnen etwas, das man nicht zählen kann. Dazu gehören viele Bezeichnungen für Lebensmittel und viele abstrakte Begriffe.

! Auch die Nomen ***furniture, homework, information*** und ***news*** sind nicht zählbar – anders als ihre deutschen Entsprechungen.

That's too much **homework**. I can't do it.
Das sind zu viele **Hausaufgaben**. Ich kann sie nicht machen.

◂ Die zugehörigen **Begleiter, Verben und Pronomen** stehen immer **im Singular**.

Would you like a glass of **milk**.
Möchtest du **ein Glas Milch**?

That's a useful piece of **information**.
Das ist **eine** nützliche **Information**.

◂ Wenn du **bestimmte Mengen** oder eine **bestimmte Anzahl** nennen willst, musst du passende Wendungen wie ***a glass of ..., a kilo of ..., a piece of ...*** verwenden.

c) Quantifiers: *some, a lot of, many, much*

Countable nouns	Uncountable nouns
some **students** einige/ein paar ...	some **bread/information** etwas Brot/einige Informationen
a lot of **students** viele ...	a lot of **bread/information** viel Brot/viele Informationen
how many **students?** wie viele ...?	
	how much **bread/information?** wie viel Brot? / wie viele Informationen?

Die Mengenangaben *some* und *a lot of* (oder *lots of*) verwendest du sowohl mit dem **Plural von zählbaren Nomen** als auch mit **nicht zählbaren Nomen**.

many („**viele**") steht nur mit dem **Plural von zählbaren Nomen**.

much („**viel**") steht nur mit **nicht zählbaren Nomen**.

GF 4 The definite article *the* ► *GF p. 160*

Wenn ein Nomen **ganz allgemein** gebraucht wird, steht es **ohne den bestimmten Artikel** (auch, wenn ein Adjektiv davor steht).
Das gilt insbesondere für

1 For Timo and his family, life is exciting at the moment. ... ist **das** Leben im Moment aufregend.

1 **abstrakte Begriffe** wie *life, history, health, quality*

2 Clean air is important to health.
Saubere Luft ist wichtig für **die** Gesundheit.

2 **Stoffbezeichnungen** wie *air, oil, gold*

3 American students do lots of extracurricular activities.

3 **Nomen im Plural** (hier: *students*).

1a At the FFA meeting Timo learned a lot about the life **of Missouri farmers**.
... über das Leben der Farmer in Missouri.

2a The Schmidts are happy that the air **in Hermann** is clean.
... die Luft in Hermann

◄ Solche Nomen stehen jedoch **mit bestimmtem Artikel**, wenn sie **näher bestimmt** sind, z.B. durch eine *of*-Fügung oder einen Relativsatz.

GF 5 Talking about the future ► *GF p. 161*

a) REVISION The *will*-future

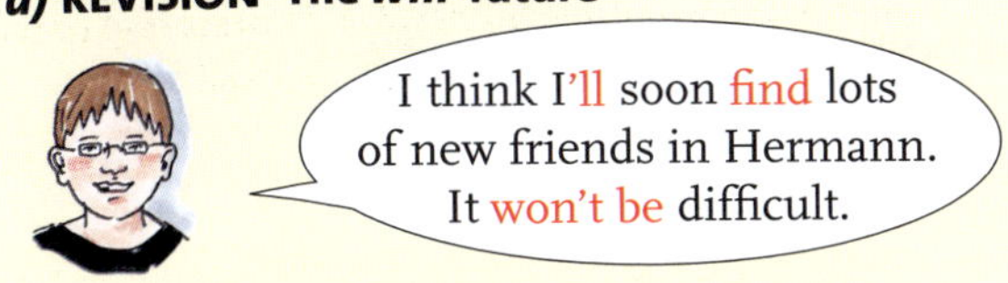

Timo is 14. He'll be 15 next year.
The weather report says that it will be warm and sunny tomorrow.

◄ Mit dem *will-future* kannst du **Vermutungen** und **Vorhersagen** über die Zukunft äußern.
Vermutungen fangen oft mit *I think, I'm sure* oder *maybe* an.
Bei Vorhersagen geht es oft um Dinge, die man nicht beeinflussen kann (das Alter; das Wetter).

Tea or coffee? – I think I'll have tea, please. Those exercises look difficult. I'll help you with them.

◄ Das *will-future* verwendest du auch für **spontane Entschlüsse**, die vorher nicht geplant waren (z.B. Hilfsangebote, Versprechen).

b) REVISION The *going to*-future

Timo Are you going to be a farmer like your dad, Jake.
Jake No, I'm not. I'm going to be a teacher.

◄ Mit dem *going to-future* kannst du über **Vorhaben** und **Pläne** für die Zukunft sprechen.

Timo's books are going to fall.

◄ Mit ***going to* + Infinitiv** kannst du auch ausdrücken, dass etwas **wahrscheinlich gleich passieren** wird.
Es gibt dafür schon deutliche **Anzeichen** (hier: die Bücher oben auf dem Stapel, die schon wackeln).

c) The present progressive with future meaning

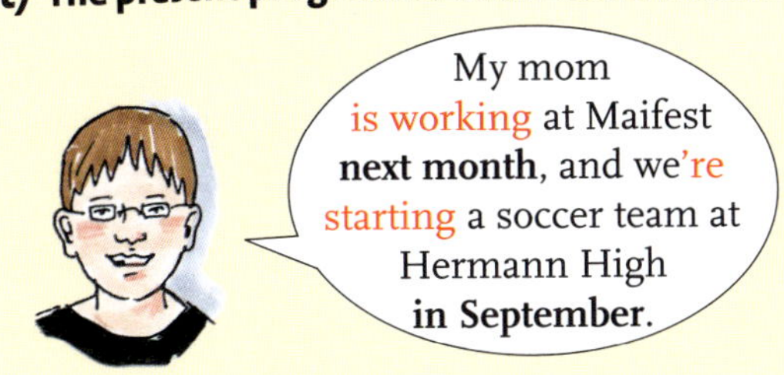

◄ **Feste Pläne** und **Verabredungen** kannst du auch mit dem *present progressive* ausdrücken. Dabei muss klar sein, dass es sich um etwas Zukünftiges handelt, z.B. durch eine Zeitangabe wie *next month, in September, on Friday, at the weekend, tomorrow*.
(Manchmal wird diese Verwendung des *present progressive* auch ***diary future***, deutsch „Kalender-Zukunft", genannt, weil es sich oft um Verabredungen handelt, die man schon in seinen Terminkalender eingetragen hat.)

Unit 4

GF 6 *since* and *for* (German 'seit')

► GF p. 162

a) The present perfect with *since* and *for*

Du kannst das *present perfect* verwenden, um über einen **Zustand** zu sprechen, der in der Vergangenheit begonnen hat und jetzt noch andauert.

! Wenn du sagen willst, **seit wann** oder **wie lange** der Zustand bereits andauert, musst du aufpassen – es gibt zwei englische Wörter für das deutsche „seit":

◄ 1 Mit *since* gibt du einen **Zeit**punkt an *(since 2001; since May; since 12 o'clock)*.
***since* + Zeitpunkt** drückt also aus, **seit wann** ein Zustand andauert.

◄ 2 Mit *for* gibst du einen **Zeit**raum an *(for years; for a month; for a long time)*.
***for* + Zeitraum** drückt also aus, **wie lange** ein Zustand bereits andauert.

We**'ve lived** in this house since 2004.
Wir **wohnen** seit 2004 in diesem Haus.

I**'ve had** my computer for three years.
Ich **habe** meinen Computer schon seit drei Jahren.

! Achtung:
Im **Deutschen** benutzt man meist das **Präsens**:
*Wir **wohnen** seit ... / Ich **habe** ... seit ...*

Im **Englischen** muss das ***present perfect*** stehen:
*We**'ve lived** ... since ... / I**'ve had** ... for ...*

***since* + Zeitpunkt** | ***for* + Zeitraum**

Madison and her mom are in the car on the way to the CNN studios. **It's 8.20.**

They**'ve been** in the traffic jam since 8 o'clock. ... seit 8 Uhr.

They**'ve been** in the traffic jam for 20 minutes. ... seit 20 Minuten.

How long **have** you **lived** in Atlanta?
– Since 2005. / For a few years.

Wie lange **wohnt** ihr in Atlanta?
– Seit 2005. / Seit ein paar Jahren.

Mit ***How long ...?*** + *present perfect* kannst du fragen, seit wann oder wie lange ein Zustand schon andauert.